ENDLESS VOW

Soen Nakagawa Roshi

ENDLESS VOW

The Zen Path of Soen Nakagawa

presented
with an Introduction by
Eido Tai Shimano

compiled and translated by
Kazuaki Tanahashi
and
Roko Sherry Chayat

SHAMBHALA
Boston & London
1996

Shambhala Publications, Inc.
Horticultural Hall
300 Massachusetts Avenue
Boston, Massachusetts 02115

9 8 7 6 5 4 3 2 1

First Edition

Printed in the United States of America

☻ This edition is printed on acid-free paper that meets
the American National Standards Institute Z39.48 Standard.

Distributed in the United States by Random House, Inc.,
and in Canada by Random House of Canada Ltd

Library of Congress Cataloging-in-Publication Data

Nakagawa, Sōen, 1907–
    Endless vow: the Zen path of Soen Nakagawa / presented with an introduction by Eido Tai Shimano, compiled and translated by Kazuaki Tanahashi and Roko Sherry Chayat.
        p.   cm.
    Translation of collection of Sōen Nakagawa's literary works.
    ISBN 1-57062-162-4 (alk. paper)
    1. Zen Buddhism. 2. Zen poetry, Japanese—Translations into English. 3. Nakagawa, Sōen, 1907– —Translations into English.
    I. Tanahashi, Kazuaki, 1933– . II. Chayat, Sherry. III. Title.
BQ9266.N33   1996   95-25753
294.3′927′092—dc20   CIP

CONTENTS

PREFACE

by Kazuaki Tanahashi

Zen Master Soen Nakagawa was a key figure in the transmission of Zen Buddhism from Japan to the Western world. As abbot of the historic Ryutaku Monastery, he trained monks and lay practitioners. Among them were Robert Aitken and Philip Kapleau, who later became two of the first Westerners to teach Zen in the United States. Soen Roshi had a major impact upon Paul Reps, Maurine Stuart, Peter Matthiessen, Louis Nordstrom, Charlotte Joko Beck, and a great number of other Westerners whom he taught in and outside of Japan.

Soen Nakagawa was also an extraordinary poet. In Japan his haiku are renowned, even though no substantial collection of his work has been made available to the general public. Because he did not wish his anthologies to receive wide circulation in his lifetime, all four collections of his poems were published privately, in limited editions, for small circles of readers.

We have selected materials for this book largely from those four collections: *Shigan* (Coffin of Poems), 1936; *Meihen* (Life Anthology), 1949; *Henkairoku* (Journal of a Wide World) with *Koun-sho* (Ancient Cloud Selection), 1981; and *Hokoju* (Long-Lasting Dharma Light), published posthumously in 1985. These selections are now presented in English for the first time.

We also used Soen Roshi's own English translations of certain poems, and several translations by Eido Tai Shimano Roshi that appeared in the *Soen Roku: The Sayings and Doings of Master Soen*, published in 1986 by the Zen Studies Society, and in *Namu*

Dai Bosa: A Transmission of Zen Buddhism to America, edited by
Louis Nordstrom and including works by Nyogen Senzaki, Soen
Nakagawa, and Eido Shimano (New York: Theatre Arts Books,
1976). Some of the poems in our book were also taken from un-
published letters and from Soen Roshi's calligraphy scrolls and
panels in the collection of International Dai Bosatsu Zendo and
the New York Zendo. *Mitta Yoko* (Lingering Fragrance of the
Master of Mitta Hut), a Japanese collection of biographical studies and memoirs about Soen Nakagawa published in 1989, has
been a valuable source as well.

A sensitive and perceptive observer, Soen Roshi kept a journal
in which he recorded his insights and experiences as a Zen monk,
along with poems and drawings. He also wrote numerous letters,
particularly to his dear friend the Venerable Nyogen Senzaki, who
was the first Zen teacher to reside in the United States. We have
included excerpts from Monk Soen's letters to Nyogen Senzaki
written before and after World War II. These are especially significant, since they illustrate formative periods not only in Soen
Roshi's life, but in the establishment of Zen in the United States.
Although some of these letters were brought out by Eido Tai
Shimano Roshi in *Zen Bunka,* a publication of Hanazono University, Kyoto, this is the first time they have been made available in
English.

The selections presented in *Endless Vow: The Zen Path of Soen
Nakagawa* are arranged in chronological order, reflecting four
periods in Soen Roshi's life: Ascetic Practice, Early Years as
Abbot, Teaching in the West, and Increasing Seclusion.

All translations of the haiku (but not the free-verse poems)
are accompanied by their Japanese texts and their romanizations.
Chinese names are represented by their Japanese syllables, according to Soen Roshi's own usage; the Chinese forms are provided in the glossary. When referring to twentieth-century Japanese individuals, we used given names followed by family names,
in the Western order. For earlier masters we have placed the most
familiar name first: for example, Joshu Jushin and Basho Matsuo.
Diacritical marks are used only in the romanized haiku and in
the glossary terms. We followed the traditional East Asian way of

counting when referring to people's ages, in which someone is one year old at birth and gains a year each New Year's Day.

I proposed the creation of this book to Eido Tai Shimano Roshi and Roko Sherry Chayat during our participation in the national conference "One Hundred Years of Zen in America," which was organized by the Zen Center of Syracuse in 1993. Eido Roshi, abbot of International Dai Bosatsu Zendo Kongo-ji and New York Zendo Shobo-ji, was Soen Roshi's closest disciple and principal Dharma successor. He is the executor of all of Soen Nakagawa's and Nyogen Senzaki's poems, essays, journal entries, letters, and calligraphy. Roko, spiritual leader of the Zen Center of Syracuse Hoen-ji, was a resident at Dai Bosatsu Zendo during the early years of its establishment. She trained under Soen Roshi and Eido Roshi there and at the New York Zendo, and in 1992 Eido Roshi acknowledged her as a Dharma Teacher in a ceremony at Dai Bosatsu Zendo. Although I did not have the chance to meet the legendary Soen Nakagawa, I have admired his poems enormously for many years, and it has been my dream to translate his work and present it to English readers.

After our initial discussions at the conference in Syracuse, Eido Roshi graciously offered to provide all available materials and his assistance to the project. In consultation with him, Roko and I selected materials for translation. She and I worked together at Dai Bosatsu Zendo, in Syracuse, and in Berkeley, and then reviewed and refined the translations with Eido Roshi at Dai Bosatsu Zendo. Roshi continued to write, expand, and polish the introduction, working with Roko over a one-year period. He also went through hundreds of his teacher's calligraphic scrolls, panels, and drawings with us to select works for illustration.

I am grateful for the opportunity to collaborate with Eido Roshi and Roko on this project. The three of us worked very well together. Using a remarkable set of primary sources, I believe we have captured the spirit of this eccentric and genuine Zen person.

The staff of International Dai Bosatsu Zendo provided wonderful support during our collaboration. We would like to express our special appreciation to Seiko Susan Morningstar for her invaluable help with early drafts of the introduction, and to

Sayoko Matsuda for her careful and dedicated copying of the original materials in Japanese. We would also like to thank the members of the Syracuse Zen Center for their enthusiasm and support.

October 1995
Berkeley, California

ENDLESS VOW

DAI BOSATSU MANDALA
A PORTRAIT OF SOEN NAKAGAWA

by Eido Tai Shimano

We join spokes together in a wheel,
but it is the center hole
that makes the wagon move.

We shape clay into a pot,
but it is the emptiness inside
that holds whatever we want.

We hammer wood for a house,
but it is the inner space
that makes it livable.

We work with being,
but non-being is what we use.

—*Tao Te Ching*, chap. 11
  (translated by Stephen Mitchell)

Although this book focuses on the poetry of Soen Nakagawa
Roshi, it is more than a selection of poems by a man who has
been called the Basho of the twentieth century. *Endless Vow: The
Zen Path of Soen Nakagawa* is an invitation to enter a mandala—
not a two- or three-dimensional one, but a mandala of what Soen
Roshi used to call Endless Dimension Universal Life.

A mandala is usually a visual representation of the intercon-
nectedness of the whole cosmos. It includes form and nonform,
being and nonbeing. Through the mysterious and subtle interweaving of action and reaction, an entity is created, yet it is without any fixed identity. The above quotation from the *Tao Te
Ching* beautifully describes the workings of a mandala.

From an ordinary perspective, events appear to be random; life appears to be chaos. But from the perspective of a mandala, things are as they are. Everything is perfect as it is. There is no coincidence. Things, people, and events might appear chaotic, but we often sense an uncanny appropriateness. There is an underlying pattern, one to which we unwittingly refer when we say, "That's the way it goes."

In this mandala, the esoteric and exoteric merge. There is no boundary between east and west; life and death are not two separate and distinct matters. Thus, although Soen Roshi passed away in 1984, he is vividly alive.

More than one thousand years ago a man named Gyoki Bosatsu (d. 749 CE), who was said to be an incarnation of Manjushri Bodhisattva, was traveling all over Japan. He went to an uninhabited place now known as Mount Dai Bosatsu, near Mount Fuji, where he erected a small one-room shrine to the deity called the Dai Bosatsu (Great Bodhisattva) Daigongen. A *daigongen* is a manifestation of Dharmakaya Buddha who appears in different forms, such as Kanzeon Bodhisattva, to guide people from ignorance to clarity. As a result of Gyoki Bosatsu's presence on that mountain, the local people began holding a ceremony honoring the Dai Bosatsu Daigongen every twenty-first day of the month.

In 1931, when the twenty-four-year-old Soen Nakagawa went to live there as a newly ordained monk, that monthly ritual was still being conducted. It was Monk Soen, living alone in a hut he called Dainichi-an (*Dainichi* is Japanese for "Vairocana Buddha"), who created the Dai Bosatsu mantra, "Namu dai bosa," which means to become one with the boundless Bodhisattva spirit that is our intrinsic nature. The echo of his solitary chanting resounded; its energy emanated throughout the world, resonating and intermingling with that of many others in the endless dimensional Dai Bosatsu mandala, whether seen or not, whether heard or not, whether realized or not.

Monk Soen began chanting "Namu dai bosa" on Mount Dai Bosatsu in Japan, and the forcefield of his energy soon reached America. He had been writing many poems and essays, which were hand-printed in a limited edition of about three hundred copies titled *Shigan* (Coffin of Poems). An editor of the women's magazine *Fujin Koron*, published in Tokyo, happened to see a copy and liked the work very much; with Monk Soen's permission, she printed some of the poems and essays, along with a preface in which she introduced the young monk as a "genius poet," in the November 1934 issue of the magazine.

One of the subscribers to *Fujin Koron* was Shubin Tanahashi, who lived in Los Angeles. She read Monk Soen's writings, was very impressed by them, and showed them to her teacher, the Venerable Nyogen Senzaki, who sent a letter of appreciation to the young poet-monk. Thus began a period of intense correspondence that ended only with Senzaki's death in 1958.

Nyogen Senzaki was the first Zen monk to be a resident teacher in the United States. He and the renowned scholar Daisetz Teitaro Suzuki were both students of Soyen Shaku, the first Zen master to come to America. Soyen Shaku presented a historic lecture on karma (previously translated by D. T. Suzuki, then twenty-three years old) at the World's Parliament of Religions in Chicago in 1893, and he returned in 1905 for a longer visit, staying with Mrs. Alexander Russell in San Francisco and giving talks on Buddhism at several locations in the United States.

According to the records of the town clerk of Fukaura-cho, Aomori, Nyogen Senzaki was born on October 5, 1876, as the first son of the Senzaki family. He was named Aizo. Due to his rather exotic appearance, many stories were spread regarding his origins. Even his grandmother would tell him, "You were abandoned as a child, and a fisherman from Sakhalin Island, Siberia, brought you here." At the age of five, Aizo lost his mother, and was sent to a Pure Land Buddhist temple where his grandfather was abbot. On April 8, 1895—Buddha's birthday—he was ordained and given the name Nyogen. He was nineteen. The following year he went to Kamakura and practiced at Engaku-ji under Soyen Shaku Roshi. In a letter written to his teacher in the early part of the twentieth century, he described those early years:

I am positive that my years at my grandfather's temple cultivated my Buddhist faith. When I was sixteen, my grandfather passed away.

Soyen Shaku

Just before his death he told me, "Even though you have told me that you want to become a monk, when I look at the way Buddhism is now in Japan, I am afraid you may regret it. So think it over."

After his death, I went to school and then prepared for medical school. During my preparations, I thought about how I had been supported by the offerings of others while living at my grandfather's temple. I thought if I didn't return to society what I had received, I would be terribly punished.

In junior high school, I read the autobiography of Benjamin Franklin, and I imitated his method for spiritual growth: Every night I would reflect on what I did during the day, and I was surprised by how many times I did the wrong thing. My days were without any peace. I lost my self-confidence. For a short while I was drawn to puritanical Christianity. Then I happened to meet a haiku poet, and learned about the life of Basho; this led me to study Zen Buddhism. One day, while preparing to enter medical school, I read the story of how Tokusan burned the volume of *Diamond Sutra* commentaries he had been studying. It was this story that confirmed me in my decision to become a Zen Buddhist monk. I was ordained at a Soto Zen Buddhist temple, since there was no Rinzai Zen temple in the area. The following year I saw you [Soyen Shaku], and that was the true turning point of my life. Although I have had the good fortune to have received *jukai* [the Buddhist precepts] twice, once when I was ordained and once again from Unsho Risshi, if I had not had the chance to meet you, it would not be possible for me to be settled in the way that I am now. Cultivating the root of the precepts, radiating the light of the precepts are all due to you. . . .

I have no way to express my gratitude to you. Because of your guidance, my vow is unshakable. No matter what happens, I will continue on the Buddha's way with The Great Vows for All.

Nyogen Senzaki followed his teacher to the United States, arriving in Seattle in 1905, and he worked for a time in the Russell home. He then took a series of odd jobs, living first in San Francisco and later in Los Angeles. In a letter of around 1917 to a brother monk, Kishu, he wrote:

Although I was Soyen Shaku's worst student, my *bodhicitta* never weakened. This, at least, the Roshi knows. Perhaps you can ask Chusan to take this letter to Roshi and tell him that Senzaki is still alive.

Nowadays I work from seven PM throughout the night as a telephone operator and bookkeeper for this hotel. Then from seven AM to eleven AM I work as housekeeper, with three American women and one Italian man as assistants. The only time I can sleep is from two PM to six PM, and when it is too busy, sometimes I don't sleep for two or three days. Between two AM and five AM, the telephone rings less often, and during that time I study.

Ever since I came to America, I have worked like a machine. Nevertheless, I am still having financial problems. Every day, using the typewriter, I write thirty or forty letters. The telephone switchboard is not only busy, but requires my full attention. On top of all this, about two hundred people are living in this hotel. Sometimes the couples fight, and I have to talk to them. Sometimes I assist the house detective in catching a thief. Other times I have to dress up and go to the theater with some of the guests. Last night someone came in drunk, so I hit him and took him to bed. And on and on. I work so hard; why can't I seem to save any money? My debts increase every month, so that I cannot be independent with my own business.

Nyogen Senzaki did not begin teaching until after Soyen Shaku's death in 1919, and lived in virtual obscurity, unlike Dr. Suzuki, who is considered the most important figure in the transmission of Zen to the West in the first half of the twentieth century. Dr. Suzuki was highly regarded in the Japanese Zen establishment. In America he spent most of his time on the East Coast, teaching at Columbia University. He published more than one hundred and thirty books in English and in Japanese before his death in 1966 at the age of ninety-five. For the Venerable Senzaki, however, what was of primary importance was not an intellectual understanding of Buddhism, but the consistent practice of *zazen*. Hoping the United States could offer a fresh start for Zen, which he felt had grown stale and decadent in Japan, he left the Zen establishment behind. He called himself a mushroom monk with no official standing; nevertheless, he played a pioneering role in the development of Zen in the West. His impact was profound, and his commentaries, essays, and poems in English—published in *The Iron Flute; Zen Flesh, Zen Bones; Zen and Buddhism; On Zen Meditation; Namu Dai Bosa: A Transmission of Zen Buddhism to America;* and *Like a Dream, Like a Fantasy*—remain influential and beloved works. Except for one trip back to Japan, the Venerable Senzaki remained on the West Coast until his death in 1958.

Mrs. Shubin Tanahashi had become the Venerable Senzaki's student in the autumn of 1932. It was also in the fall of 1932 that Monk Soen first attempted to realize his dream of an international zendo; he went on a fundraising trip to Sakhalin Island, near Siberia, where he literally searched for gold (unsuccessfully). And it was in the fall of 1932 that I was born, in Nakano Arai, Tokyo. In this eventful autumn, three individuals still unknown to each other were being woven into the Dai Bosatsu mandala; these three would be instrumental in the birth of International Dai Bosatsu Zendo.

In the spring of 1938, while living in Manchuria, Monk Soen wrote the following letter to the Venerable Senzaki:

In Japan, on Mount Dai Bosatsu, the local deity festival is held on the twenty-first day of every month. Therefore, let us set this day as Spiritual Interrelationship Day. Those who are interested in seeking the Dharma, wherever they reside on this planet: start zazen at eight PM local time, entering into samadhi, and from 8:30, listen to the spiritual broadcasting of *kenteki*, the offering of the *shakuhachi* flute. Then chant the twenty-fifth chapter of the *Lotus Sutra*, "The Great Compassionate Dharani," "Namu dai bosa," and then the dedication to the Dai Bosatsu Deity. After that, at each place have a joyous gathering. Is this not a Universal Bodhisattva occasion? What a joyous event! This Spiritual Interrelationship Garden has no specific place; rather, the entire cosmos is the garden. The members of the Dai Bosatsu group are all animate and inanimate beings. If some animate being really wants to join, he can be a member instantly, all by himself. If five or six people want to be members, that is also fine.

On the evening of the twenty-first of every month, we will go into the depths of form and nonform. For now, we call it Dai Bosatsu Deity, but fundamentally it is the *sunyata*-of-sunyata, or the profundity-of-profundity. What a liberated spirit!

Who was the young monk who wrote those prophetic words? Who was Soen Roshi? I am often asked this question, and in truth I have asked it myself every day for more than forty years. For me, Soen Nakagawa has been the biggest koan of my life. Soen Roshi was my teacher, and true to the Zen tradition, we met each other mind-to-mind, heart-to-heart, *hara*-to-hara (the lower abdomen, considered the locus of spiritual power). This unique relationship in Zen between teacher and student exists on a deep level that cannot be rationally explained. It may include love and hate, dependence and independence. There is profound and mutual recognition of a sort that goes beyond the usual human emotions. It is an uncanny bonding, a merging of identities. Because of our Dharma connection, our karma is forever intermingled. Even with this understanding, however, I cannot say definitively who Soen Roshi was.

He had many faces: he was a simple monk, a "crazy wisdom" Zen master, a genius in the arts, a spiritually realized being of the highest attainment, a dedicated student of the Dharma, a master manipulator, a troubled human being, a skillful politician, a tactful diplomat, a stupendous host, an inspired guest. He was refined yet could be wildly unpredictable; he was subtle yet could be exasperatingly vague. He used the imperturbable mask of a Zen master to hide his excruciatingly sensitive emotional life. When, toward the end, that mask was taken away, his deep suffering manifested itself in behavior that was often shocking but that freed him at last from conventions. His teacher Gempo Yamamoto Roshi used to say, "At the age of sixty, one is more efficient than at fifty; seventy is more useful than sixty; eighty is more effective than seventy. But our real life begins after we depart from the corporeal body." Soen Roshi quoted this quite often, and now I, too, believe it to be so.

When I was young, I did not think of Soen Roshi as an individual person; I often said that he was karma itself. I couldn't imagine that he would ever die. Even though his body disintegrated into the four elements more than twelve years ago, I still feel that way in my heart. From the perspective of the Dai Bosatsu mandala, he is not at all dead. In fact, the more the years pass, the more alive he seems.

Digging into my memories of Soen Roshi, I have come to have new insights about aspects of our relationship that were not apparent to me when I was younger. They are not so much from an emotional or psychological perspective, but from the Endless Dimension Universal Life vista. From this Dai Bosatsu mandala point of view, it really doesn't matter whether the contradictions are resolved or not.

This Dai Bosatsu mandala consists of innumerable buddhas, bodhisattvas, and ancestors from both the East and the West who played a role in the formation of a Dharma phenomenon in "the land of liberty." There are at least four generations that I can name as part of this mandala. The first generation was that of Soyen Shaku and Gempo Roshi. The second includes Nyogen Senzaki, Soen Roshi, Shubin Tanahashi, Chester Carlson, and others mentioned in this narrative. The third is my generation; the fourth is the current Sangha, perhaps including those who are reading this now.

In 1972, when I was installed as the abbot of New York Zendo Shobo-ji and officially acknowledged as his Dharma heir, Soen Roshi told me, "When the time is right, you have my permission to use my poetry, calligraphy, letters, and articles, as well as Nyogen Senzaki's correspondence and essays, for translation and publication in European languages."

Soen Roshi's path was remarkably clear from his youngest days. Born on March 19, 1907, in Keelung, Formosa (now Taiwan), he was the first of three sons. His parents named him Motoi, after the first Chinese character in the name Keelung. When he was young his father, an army doctor, passed away. His mother was in her midtwenties when she was widowed; not long afterward her second son, Tamotsu, died. Her relationship with her oldest son was a particularly close and significant one.

From the beginning, Motoi exhibited a brilliant, artistic, and playful spirit. One day, he and his classmates at Hiroshima Junior High School pooled their pocket money to purchase a recording of Beethoven's *Ninth Symphony*, which had just been made available in Japan. Overwhelmed by the experience of listening to it, he shivered for three days afterward; throughout his life, he was passionately fond of this and other masterpieces by Beethoven.

As a descendant of a samurai family and the eldest son of an army doctor, it was assumed that he would pursue a military career, but he was rejected from military service because of a mistaken medical diagnosis of a perforated eardrum. Instead he entered First Academy in Tokyo, where one of his roommates was a boy who would later become Yamada Koun Roshi, and who began his own Zen path due to an inspiring encounter with Monk Soen in Manchuria during the 1930s.

Why did Motoi become Monk Soen? The loss of his father when he was quite young may have had a lot to do with his decision to renounce worldly life. Another factor may have been that he often felt unable to communicate with people in the usual ways. He was more comfortable in the company of Goethe, Dante, Schopenhauer, Beethoven, Mozart, and Basho than he was with his fellow students. For him, those authors and composers were vibrantly alive; they were speaking to him directly. In *Shigan,* his first published work, he wrote:

> I was a freshman at First Academy, searching for something
> worthwhile to which to dedicate my life. Unless I found a truly
> worthy thing to do with my life, whatever I did would be
> meaningless—thus I thought. But I could not find it in the everyday
> world at that time. I was deeply disappointed, frustrated, and
> depressed. . . . One day in the library, I was reading Schopenhauer,
> and one page shocked me. My mind ceased searching. It became
> lucid and tranquil. Schopenhauer said, "In the *real* world, it is
> impossible to attain true happiness, final and eternal contentment.
> For these are visionary flowers in the air; mere fantasies. In truth,
> they can never be actualized. In fact, they must not be actualized.
> Why? If such ideals were to be actualized, the search for the real

meaning of our existence would cease. If that happened, it would be the spiritual end of our being, and life would seem too foolish to live."

After high school, he was accepted at the prestigious Tokyo Imperial University, where he read widely in Buddhist scriptures, the Bible, and Japanese and Western classics. While in college, he lived for three years at a nearby Jodo Shu (Pure Land) temple, Gangyo-ji. From his studies in Buddhism, Basho, and Rikyu, and from his engagement in the art of the tea ceremony, his knowledge of Rinzai Zen Buddhism deepened; he practiced zazen regularly, organizing a *zazenkai* (Zen sitting group for laypeople) for his fellow students, as he had at First Academy. According to his brother, Sonow Nakagawa, it was while preparing his graduation paper, on Basho's *The Monkey's Raincoat*, that Motoi first decided to become a Zen monk.

Although he was a brilliant scholar, artist, and poet, he knew in his heart that academic or artistic achievements alone would not be sufficiently meaningful. He could have gone on to do many things in the world of scholarship; he could have had the highest position in some worldly endeavor. Even as a child, his intuitive nature and his creative talents were clearly far above the usual level. During his college days, he led his life as though he were a contemporary of poets like Basho or Issa or Saigyo. At that time in Japan, people were nostalgic for that ancient tradition; here was a twentieth-century man talking, creating, and behaving like those poets.

But the Dai Bosatsu mandala was already beckoning. There happened to be a Rinzai Zen temple, Shorin-ji, near Tokyo University, where he was now in graduate school; at Shorin-ji, Keigaku Katsube Roshi held zazen meetings that were open to the public. That is how Soen Nakagawa met his ordination teacher. Keigaku Roshi was the abbot of Kogaku-ji, the monastery founded by the great Bassui; this monastery just happened to be about two or three hours' walk from Mount Dai Bosatsu. It "just happened" the way it was meant to be. Because of Soen Nakagawa's great determination and dedication to the Dharma, the Dai Bosatsu mandala could reveal and manifest itself through him.

After finishing his graduate studies in 1931, he told his mother, who had been supporting him while he was at the university, that he had decided to shave his head. She cried, begging him not to throw everything away, but on March 19, 1931—his twenty-fourth birthday—he was ordained by Keigaku Roshi at Kogaku-ji.

Only a few monks were in training at Kogaku-ji, so the daily routine was more flexible than at other monasteries. Monk Soen was able to go on solitary retreats on Mount Dai Bosatsu. People saw something unusual in him; they realized right away that he was no ordinary monk and supported his desire to do solitary practice. His becoming a monk had nothing to do with wanting a career as a priest, so he was able to avoid the usual requirements of monastic training for the priesthood. If his goal had been to get a certificate to become a priest and, eventually, an abbot, he would have had to observe all the monastic rules, but for him, conducting funerals and other rituals was not at all what being ordained was about.

It so happened that the haiku master Dakotsu Iida, who was regarded as one of the best haiku poets of his time, was also living near Mount Dai Bosatsu; Monk Soen sent some of his haiku to him, and Dakotsu Sensei published them in his celebrated journal, *Unmo*. He met with the young poet-monk and had an important influence on his work.

In 1935, Keigaku Roshi's zazenkai in Tokyo was about to begin a weekend *sesshin* (an intensive meditation retreat). There was no *keisaku* (the encouragement stick used on students' shoulders to relieve stiff muscles and increase alertness), so Keigaku Roshi asked Monk Soen to go to the neighboring temple, Hakusan Dojo, to borrow one.

Gempo Yamamoto Roshi, who was then sixty-seven years old, happened to be conducting a weekend sesshin there at the time. Even though he was only borrowing a keisaku, Monk Soen stayed to listen to Gempo Roshi's *teisho* (a talk conveying a master's understanding of Zen). He had often gone to listen to the teisho of various teachers. Some he found exciting and clear, but they didn't seem to penetrate his heart. Initially, listening to Gempo Roshi, he didn't understand very much, but later, he felt as if he had been bathing in a hot spring: the warmth pervaded his heart for many days.

Monk Soen brought the keisaku back from the weekend ses-shin at Keigaku Roshi's place, and some time afterward he went again to hear Gempo Roshi. This time, the teisho was on the *Gateless Gate (Mumonkan)*, a famous koan collection. Monk Soen happened to be sitting right in front of Gempo Roshi, and he felt as if he alone were being addressed. He never forgot what Gempo Roshi said, quoting Mumon: "If you do practice, it must be genuine practice; if you get insight, it must be true insight."

The Dai Bosatsu mandala had begun to exert its influence, subtly arranging people, events, and situations. To paraphrase from chapter 17 of the *Tao Te Ching*:

> When the mandala governs, the people are hardly aware that
> it exists. . . .
> The mandala doesn't talk, it acts.
> When its work is done,
> The people say, "Amazing:
> We did it, all by ourselves!"

In 1935, soon after hearing Gempo Roshi's teisho, Monk Soen had a private meeting with him. Just a year later, Gempo Roshi invited the young monk to go to Manchuria with him and to practice at his temple, Ryutaku-ji, in Mishima City, on the other side of Mount Fuji. Upon losing Monk Soen, Keigaku Roshi cried, "Gempo is a thief!"

The administrators of Ryutaku-ji's head temple, Myoshin-ji, in Kyoto, wanted to establish a branch temple in Manchuria, where Japan was expanding its territories. They appointed Gempo Roshi to be the founder, and Monk Soen accompanied him, traveling back and forth through the Korean peninsula by train and boat.

Monk Soen was strongly drawn to Gempo Roshi; nevertheless, in many of his letters to Nyogen Senzaki from Manchuria and Ryutaku-ji, he complained about his teacher, describing again and again his contradictory emotions—a not uncommon phe-nomenon among Zen students. I must confess that I, in turn, have had mixed feelings toward Soen Roshi. My admiration, re-

Gempo Yamamoto Roshi, 1951

spect, and love for him are firm and profound; yet mixed in with
those feelings at various times have been disappointment, criticism, and doubt. I have also engendered such emotions in my
students, and I understand them. I can't help but think these
mixed feelings must be part of the transmission from ancient to
modern times, from East to West.

Although nearly blind, Gempo Roshi was a charismatic Zen
master renowned throughout Japan for his wisdom and understanding of human nature, and for his powerful Zen calligraphy.
Japan's surrender, ending World War II in the Pacific, was in part
due to his influence. In April 1945 the prime minister, General
Kantaro Suzuki, was searching for a way to end the war. He asked
Gempo Roshi for his advice in a secret meeting in Tokyo. Gempo

Roshi encouraged him to pursue the path of surrender and to accept the reality of defeat. Gempo Roshi said, "We must endure what is hard to endure and persevere in that which is hard to persevere in." Those very words were used in the emperor's radio broadcast announcing the unconditional surrender of Japan at twelve noon on August 15, 1945. It was at that secret meeting that Gempo Roshi also advised the prime minister that the emperor should not rule or take part in politics but should be viewed as "the sun shining in the sky," as a national symbol. This became part of article 1 of Japan's new constitution, in which the function of the emperor is defined as "a symbol of the nation."

After the war, many important government officials met with Gempo Roshi for his advice. Among them was Shigeru Yoshida, who was the prime minister who signed the peace treaty. In October 1947, Gempo Roshi was invited to be abbot of Myoshin-ji, the highest honor in the Rinzai Zen establishment. He accepted the post; however, he stepped down four months later and returned to Ryutaku-ji.

Ryutaku-ji (Dragon Swamp Temple) is a small but prestigious monastery in Mishima, located near Mount Fuji at the top of Izu peninsula. It was founded in 1771 by the great Zen master Hakuin Ekaku, who is regarded as the restorer of Rinzai Zen, which had been in a state of decline. He was so influential that even today, monks and nuns of the Rinzai School are regarded as his descendants. Hakuin was abbot of Shoin-ji, in Hara; when his disciples proposed purchasing the Ryutaku-ji site as a mountain training center, he appointed Torei Enji, his most senior disciple, to oversee its establishment. Gempo Roshi brought new life to Ryutaku-ji, which had lost its accreditation as a monastic training center in the intervening years; this official standing was restored in 1941.

Even at Ryutaku-ji, Monk Soen went his own way, continuing his solitary retreats and traveling more than the other monks. They were often frustrated by his refusal to conform to the established order of daily life; he wouldn't accept any position in the running of the monastery and often sat all day and all night, ignoring the official schedule. His strict diet, which he had devised for himself while living in his hut on Mount Dai Bosatsu, made it difficult for him to take his meals with the other monks. He ate no cooked food. When traveling by train or boat, he took no meals in restaurants and bought no prepared food; he would pick up banana peels and apple cores others had thrown away, wash them, and save them for his meals.

At one point, several senior monks went to Gempo Roshi to complain about this very independent and seemingly arrogant monk, suggesting he be sent elsewhere for "retraining." Since Ryutaku-ji had just recently been officially recognized as a training center, they thought perhaps another monastery could exert a firmer influence on his conduct. Gempo Roshi's reply was, "There is no other roshi anywhere in Japan who could deal with someone like Soen."

Here is an example of how he himself dealt with his wayward student: One day, Gempo Roshi asked Monk Soen to accompany him to the temple where he had been ordained, Sekkei-ji, on Shikoku Island. Gempo Roshi went there quite often to express his gratitude to his deceased ordination teacher. On this occasion, the war had just ended and traveling by train was nearly impossible. Overwhelming crowds of people would wait for days for trains, which ran infrequently and unpredictably. When a train did arrive, there would be a mad rush not only for seats but for standing room or a place to hold on in a doorway. Gempo Roshi and Monk Soen found a spot in an aisle. Gempo Roshi sat on the floor, squeezing his body into an uncomfortably small spot. Monk Soen, however, sat in full lotus on the floor. Many people admired his zazen concentration. On the way back, there were the same overcrowded conditions. Upon returning to Ryutaku-ji, Gempo Roshi called the monk to his room and scolded in a thundering voice, "What's the matter with you? Zazen is not a performance! Under such circumstances as we had, you must think of others and make yourself as small as you can. *That* is zazen. Get out of here!" Monk Soen, who had been so admired, left Gempo Roshi's room humiliated and angry. He went to a pond at the Mishima Shrine and jumped into the water. Mulling over his teacher's words, he understood what Gempo Roshi meant; he returned to Ryutaku-ji and apologized.

Despite such incidents, Gempo Roshi treasured Monk Soen as a student and went out of his way to accommodate him. He even invited Mrs. Nakagawa to live at Ryutaku-ji, knowing how close Monk Soen and his mother were. In 1942 he had a small house built for her on the monastery grounds, called the Sun-Moon Cottage, so that she could be near her beloved son.

I once asked Soen Roshi, "Why did you become a monk?" "I so badly wanted to become a monk," he answered. "But why?" "I so badly wanted to become a monk."

His vow was truly profound. The intensity of it was remarkable; one felt it immediately. Standing in front of Hakuin's grave at Ryutaku-ji when he first visited it, he composed this haiku:

Endless is my vow
under the azure sky
boundless autumn

Even when he lived within the monastic establishment, his personal dedication was unswervingly to three guiding forces: "Shu jo mu hen sei gan do" ("However innumerable all beings are, I vow to save them all"); "Namu dai bosa"; and Bassui's "What is This?"* Monk Soen wasted no time over monastery politics. He certainly had no intention of becoming Gempo Roshi's successor, yet that is what happened. Gempo Roshi had intended to make a monk named Shun-san his successor. At that time, Shun-san was regarded as the best *unsui* in Japan (*unsui* means literally, "floating cloud, running water," a metaphor for a Zen monk). After World War II, Shun-san took his own life. Gempo Roshi made another will, in which he specified that Monk Soen would be the next abbot of Ryutaku-ji. Monk Soen's reputation as unique was by then well established, and everyone acknowledged his academic credentials and his strong spiritual dedication.

Monk Soen had no idea that he had been named in Gempo Roshi's will as his successor. He found out in a most unusual

* Like Joshu's "Mu," Bassui's "What is This?" is used by Zen practitioners to probe the nature of Mind.

way. Because Gempo Roshi was in good health after celebrating his eighty-fifth birthday, a special week of jukai (precept-receiving) ceremonies was organized at Ryutaku-ji. In a letter dated 1950 to Nyogen Senzaki, Monk Soen wrote:

> One day, more than three thousand people came for jukai; on another day, four thousand came. There was one day of purification, with many prostrations, and a Dharma talk by Gempo Roshi. They all left with joyful tears.
>
> During this jukai week, Ryutaku-ji really grew spiritually settled. I received your letters almost every other day, and shared them with my Dharma friends. We put our palms together upon reading them. We are so grateful that you and Dr. Suzuki are in good health and active in the Dharma in the West.
>
> I always thought "Dharma heir" or "Zen master" were not at all important, and would have nothing to do with me. However, to my surprise, during *sozarei* [formal tea ceremony] on the last day of jukai, Rev. Sessan Amakuki announced that I would be Gempo Roshi's heir. What an irony, what a contradiction! Right now I regard this as my life koan, and I am working on it.

Sessan Amakuki was one of the first Zen priests to visit America. He did so alone, not long after the World's Parliament of Religions in 1893. He later became the chief administrator at Myoshin-ji, one of the most powerful positions in the Rinzai Zen establishment. At the time of the jukai ceremonies, he was living nearby, as the retired abbot of Tobo-ji. On that day, he stood up and said to Gempo Roshi, "Congratulations on your long life. We are so happy for you, and we are also very happy that you have found a good successor in En-San [as Monk Soen was called]. We are very pleased that Ryutaku-ji will be in his capable hands."

At that time, Monk Soen had completed his koan practice, but hearing about being designated his teacher's successor from someone else, in a public gathering, came as quite a shock. "I couldn't believe that a man like myself was going to become the

Soen Roshi's installation as abbot of Ryutaku-ji, 1951

abbot of Ryutaku-ji!" he told me, remembering that day. "It was just unbelievable!"

I asked him, "What did Gempo Roshi say to you later on?"

"He said, 'This is as it should be.'" This was Gempo Roshi's way of expressing the action of the Dai Bosatsu mandala.

In 1951, at the age of forty-five, Soen Roshi was installed as the abbot of Ryutaku-ji. Gempo Roshi died in 1961, and in 1962 Soen Roshi's mother passed away. Suddenly he had the authority and freedom to express his own unconventional ideas. His approach seemed fresh, original, and creative, and it led many students, myself among them, to believe that he was a thoroughly modern roshi. Since he had not learned the correct forms of many ceremonies, having spent most of his training days as a hermit doing solitary retreats, he was uncomfortable teaching certain traditions. For a Japanese Zen master, his attitude was quite antiestablishment. Perhaps because of the Western influences in his education, he emphasized equality. For example, rather than being served separately as other roshis were, he took his meals with the monks. He sat zazen with his monks every day; he joined them in their *takuhatsu* (the training in humility and gratitude in which the monks walk through the town asking for alms in order to give people an opportunity to practice charity). Traditional Japanese training incorporates both distinction and equality. As the saying goes, "Equality without clear distinction is not the teaching of Buddha Dharma. Distinction without absolute equality is not the teaching of Buddha Dharma either."

Among those in the mainstream Rinzai Zen establishment, Soen Roshi's behavior was considered quite eccentric, not only because of his originality, but because he was such a well-educated, well-traveled, and culturally sophisticated person. His elite education and his familiarity with Western culture and ideas both set him apart from his peers and gave him the unusual ability to move fluidly from the Japanese way in Japan to the Western way in Japan, from the Japanese way in the West to the Western way in the West.

Soen Roshi always had the courage to do what he knew was right for himself, regardless of whether it was in line with the accepted standards of the Japanese Zen community. For example, even after Soen Roshi became the abbot of Ryutaku-ji, he continued to attend sesshin with Harada Sogaku Roshi at Hosshin-ji. This was considered highly unusual behavior for a roshi and abbot of a monastery, who was supposed to have "finished" his training. A rumor was spread that Soen Roshi did not have genuine insight and therefore needed more training under Harada Roshi, who had a strong reputation in both Rinzai and Soto Zen circles for the depth and clarity of his insight. Gempo Roshi was still alive, and each time Soen Roshi returned from Hosshin-ji, he would talk about the Hosshin-ji-style sesshin, such as how the keisaku fell on the students' shoulders like pouring rain; the *kensho* (realization) acknowledgment ceremony; the classification of the participants into "those desperate for kensho," those of "medium" desire for kensho, and "others." For each class the keisaku was used accordingly. At Hosshin-ji, they had one hour in the afternoon when all students would shout "Mu" and the keisaku would strike continuously. According to Soen Roshi, Gempo Roshi said, "Our zazen practice should be more natural."

Nevertheless, Soen Roshi kept going there, and according to a letter he wrote to Nyogen Senzaki, after one sesshin he was relaxing at Amano Hashidate, considered one of the three most beautiful places in Japan, when he had one of the deepest Zen experiences of his life. He was forever grateful to Harada Roshi, and later he insisted that I attend two sesshins; I, too, am deeply grateful for having participated. To my knowledge, no other roshi in Japan had Soen Roshi's courage, faith, and enthusiasm for the Dharma. His unshakable conviction has inspired, encouraged, and guided me in my own struggles in America, and I am profoundly thankful.

This account may give readers the impression that Soen Roshi had at least four teachers: Gempo Roshi, Harada Roshi, Keigaku Roshi, and Nyogen Senzaki. Gempo Roshi was his lineage teacher; Harada Roshi provided him with great inspiration; Keigaku Roshi was his ordination teacher and first *dokusan* teacher; and Nyogen Senzaki was his karmic soulmate and, despite the geographical distance between them, his most intimate friend.

In one of his letters to the Venerable Senzaki he writes, "I have had no teacher for poetry, no teacher for Zen; as I was always called a 'genius' student, unfortunately I was always teacherless."

One might say that in the most profound sense, he was a student of Bassui, who lived seven hundred years earlier. His ordination took place at Kogaku-ji, Bassui's monastery. In almost every letter to Nyogen Senzaki, he quoted Bassui. Throughout his life, in his talks to the monks and in his writings, he would say, "After all, Bassui's 'Who is it that hears this?' is the essence of Zen Buddhism."

Soen Roshi's independent spirit, creativity, and aesthetic sensitivity were extremely attractive to me as a young monk, and I fell in love with him, as did his American students. The first time I saw him was in February 1954. A funeral service was being held for a successor of Soyen Shaku named Daikyu Mineo Roshi, who had been the retired abbot of Heirin-ji, near Tokyo, when he died at the age of ninety-five. He was such a venerable and important teacher that nearly all the roshis in Japan attended the service. I happened to be *inji* (attendant) at the time to Keizan Shirouzu, abbot of Heirin-ji, who had trained at Shogen-ji with Itsugai Kajiura Roshi.

The roshis gathered in a special room of the ancient temple of Heirin-ji. Some I already knew, some I did not. With two other attendant monks, I served them tea. Some were smoking, most were talking; no one was paying particular attention to the tea being served. Since for the most part they saw each other rarely, they were all quite excited. However, there was one young roshi who caught my attention. When I brought him a cup of tea, he placed his palms together gratefully. I bowed; he truly received the tea. He wasn't talking, wasn't smoking. It may have been that he had no friends among the other roshis, as he had become one so recently. Later, during the funeral service, his singleminded chanting also impressed me. I asked someone, "Who is that?" My friend answered, "That is the new abbot of Ryutaku-ji. Although he is only in his forties, he has already been to America." That summer, I left Heirin-ji for Ryutaku-ji. After I passed the entrance requirements, Soen Roshi invited me to take a walk with him. He asked me about the koans I had been working on and then presented me with a beautiful poem on a *shikishi* (a square panel for calligraphy):

Flapping ink-black sleeves
stepping silently in straw sandals
absorbed in thought
gazing far beyond.

Even those who found Soen Roshi too controversial had to admire his uniqueness and his brilliance. Despite his unconventional ways, he could conduct himself with utter grace and effortless poise. Because he had authentic Dharma transmission, his credentials within the Japanese monastic establishment were impeccable. In his first fifteen years as abbot, he observed the proprieties when it was necessary to do so, maintaining complete harmony with his environment. He played the part of abbot so well that I am reminded of how Dogen Zenji described himself in his *Self-Portrait:* "This mountain monk's nose is as high as a mountain." But there were many occasions when Soen Roshi perplexed and irritated his fellow priests in Japan.

Once, on a very hot day in the middle of summer, Itsugai Kajiura Roshi, abbot of Shogen-ji (who later became the abbot of Myoshin-ji), and his attendant, Sogen Yamakawa (who is now the abbot of Shogen-ji), visited Ryutaku-ji. They were shocked to see that despite the heat, a *hibachi* (used to warm the hands in cold weather) was set out. Soen Roshi gestured toward the hibachi, and when they looked inside, swimming in a bowl of water was a beautiful goldfish. It was Soen Roshi's completely original way of providing his guests with a refreshing moment of coolness on a summer day.

Having lived in America for more than three decades, I know that from a Western point of view, Soen Roshi's way of greeting his visitors could be taken as an expression of his free, poetic Zen spirit. However, from their conservative, conventional Japanese viewpoint, it was interpreted as strange and disrespectful. One must remember that at that meeting, Soen Roshi was a new roshi. Itsugai Roshi, by far his senior, was the abbot of a monastery founded by Kanzan Egen Zenji six hundred years earlier. Ryutaku-ji, although established as a temple by Hakuin Ekaku Zenji about two hundred years ago, had been a training monastery for only fifty years.

In 1965, for the ceremony commemorating the eleven hundredth year of Rinzai's death, almost all the roshis of the Rinzai School gathered in Kyoto at Tofuku-ji, which is the largest Rinzai temple. Soen Roshi proudly brought his prized teabowl, a black bowl he had bought from a street vendor in China before the war when he had visited Rinzai's pagoda. He had only paid about five cents for it; later, a tea authority told him the bowl was really precious. Soen Roshi kept the bowl in a special wooden box. On that formal occasion, he startled the assembled dignitaries by whisking powdered tea himself, rather than having his attendant do it, as is the custom.

Now we in the West might interpret this as an example of Soen Roshi's personal warmth and humility. But in Japan the tea ceremony, especially at a formal event such as this, must be carried out in the traditional manner, so that harmony is observed and everyone feels comfortable. By taking over the role of his assistant, he acted in a way that was incomprehensible to the other roshis. Through incidents like this one, he became notorious for his unconventional behavior. In America, we delighted in calling him untamed; in Japan, they called him untrained, and some turned away from him.

After making tea that day, he did something the other roshis considered even more outrageous: he asked each of them to write "Kwatz!" (Rinzai's famous shout) on the inside of the teabowl box's lid. To make this kind of request was unprecedented. Some of the roshis responded with delight, some with reluctance. Then the abbot of Myoshin-ji, Taiko Furukawa Roshi, with whom Soen Roshi was very close, wrote on the top of the lid: "No kwatz!" Many years later, I asked Soen Roshi why Itsugai Roshi's "kwatz" was missing. He told me that Itsugai Roshi had gone over to the box and had just sat there. He had not picked up the brush; he had not written anything. "That was *his* kwatz!" Soen Roshi told me. I got some insight with that!

Soen Roshi created a world far different from that of other Zen masters. It was a world where beauty, aesthetic concerns, and gestures touching the ancient heart were more important than propriety. He believed that beauty is not what is obvious but what is mysterious and hidden. Once he asked me, "Tai-san, how do you define beauty?" We think we know what beauty is, but when the question is asked, it's not so easy to answer. I said, "You are my teacher, so please define it for me." He said, "If an event is unrepeatable, that is beauty." This was his definition: beauty is unrepeatable. It is something that is so subtle that it cannot be spoken of.

As I have mentioned, Soen Roshi's identity and his aesthetic sensibility were molded by his reverence for the monk-poets of ancient Japan. In Japanese, Zen words are called *zengo*, and calligraphy is called *bokuseki*. The zengo can be understood superficially with the intellect, but their spiritual depth is revealed through zazen. The bokuseki of Zen masters not only has breathtaking beauty and power but an energy that comes from *samadhi*. Thus it endures through the centuries. Likewise, the best haiku is an expression of Zen mind; language is used to convey a concrete experience of an unforgettable, unrepeatable moment.

A popular saying often used by calligraphers for scrolls displayed in the tea ceremony alcove is "ichigo ichie," which means "an unprecedented, unrepeatable encounter." The significance and perhaps the most important and lasting effect of Soen Roshi's poetry and calligraphy may have less to do with the world of aesthetics than it does with the transmission of the Dharma to America through his encounter with Nyogen Senzaki.

In a letter dated 1948 to the Venerable Nyogen, he said: "I will cross the Pacific Ocean doing zazen, and on April 8, the day I arrive in San Francisco, I beg you to ordain me as part of the Buddha's Birthday celebration. For nearly two decades, I have lived a big mistake; if I now could become a simple monk, I couldn't be happier. This coming twenty-first day at Gangyo-ji in Tokyo, we will have our monthly Dai Bosatsu gathering. Namu dai bosa! Namu dai bosa!"

What did he mean by his "big mistake"? Perhaps he was referring to his disenchantment with the Japanese Zen establishment, to which the Venerable Nyogen no longer really belonged. In any case, to my knowledge, the requested ordination did not take place.

For years, Soen Nakagawa and Nyogen Senzaki had been trying to meet face to face. During the period just before World War II, it was almost impossible to get a passport and visa, and of course throughout the war years, it was out of the question. In 1949, Monk Soen was finally able to arrange everything. Their first-time meeting was truly an unprecedented and unrepeatable manifestation of a rare and beautiful friendship. From San Francisco

Soen Roshi in Los Angeles during his first visit to the United States, 1949

harbor they drove to Los Angeles and spent many happy weeks together chanting "Namu dai bosa, namu dai bosa."

In the spring of 1955, Soen Roshi went again to visit Nyogen Senzaki, and in October of 1956, the Venerable Nyogen returned to Japan for the first time in his fifty years abroad. He was accompanied on that visit by Kangetsu Ruth McCandless and Kokin Louise Peddeford. It was then that I met Nyogen Senzaki for the first and only time in this life. Yet through our brief encounter, our karmic connection became apparent. Soen Roshi arranged for me to become the Venerable Nyogen's attendant in America, but in 1958, before I could make the trip, we received news of Nyogen Senzaki's death. He named Soen Roshi the executor of his estate. Later that year, Soen Roshi returned to California to settle Senzaki's affairs and to move his zendo across the street to Shubin Tanahashi's house.

At that time he met Charles Gooding, one of Senzaki's students. In 1963, Mr. Gooding, who was a stockbroker, took Soen Roshi on a trip around the world. They traveled in style, staying

Nyogen Senzaki with Soen Roshi and his mother, Mrs. Nakagawa, at Ryutaku-ji

in the best hotels. Many of the haiku in this book were composed on that trip. Just as Soen Roshi had a daring and adventurous mind, immersing himself in the literature and music of East and West, he approached travel with the same enthusiasm. He was a true wanderer. Soen Roshi and I traveled together a lot. On one trip, we drove across the continent from California to Wyoming and then to Iowa, where we took a plane to New York. While we were in the car, I said to the driver, "Nature is calling."

Soen Roshi asked, "What does that mean?" I explained, and he said, "Well, that is a wonderful expression. I wish I had known about it in 1949, on my first visit to the United States!" "Why?" I asked.

"I was really excited at meeting Nyogen Senzaki. We drove together all the way from San Francisco to Los Angeles; it was a trip of six or seven hours, with only one stop at a restaurant. As we neared the city, my nature was calling, but I was too shy to mention it to Nyogen Senzaki. I became pale and covered with sweat, but I didn't know what to say. When we finally arrived at the hotel, I thought I could at last find a toilet, but there was a whole crowd of Senzaki's students waiting for us. I had to be introduced to them one by one, shaking hands and listening to their welcoming remarks. I was so uncomfortable! Finally I made it to the bathroom. Now I am very grateful to know that I can say, 'My nature is calling.'" This became one of Soen Roshi's favorite expressions.

Once Soen Roshi and I took a boat from Yokohama to Seattle and then went from there to New York by train. It was winter, and we were sharing a sleeping compartment. One morning at dawn we looked out at Nebraska and everything, the entire world, was completely flat and white with snow, and then suddenly the huge, red ball of the sun rolled up over the horizon. We were rolling along, the sun was rolling up, and he composed a haiku that includes the mystical mantra from the esoteric tradition venerating Vairocana Buddha (Dainichi in Japanese):

On abi ra
un ken yuki no
yo ake kana!

Snow everywhere
first morning light
On abi ra un ken sowa ka!

Soen Roshi was born in the year of the sheep, and I was born in the year of the monkey, so he and I had the same protecting deity, Vairocana Buddha. Looking at the huge red disk appearing over the pure white expanse outside our window, he said to me, "That's for both of us." In the esoteric mandalas, Vairocana is at the center of the cosmic universe.

Our trip from Japan to Seattle had taken two weeks. One night on board ship he woke me up, saying, "Let's go outside." I was very sleepy. It was a chilly evening and completely dark; great waves were crashing over the deck. The boat was approaching land. Soen Roshi had his bell, and he said, "Let's chant together, 'Namu dai bosa.'"

There was nobody around. Our shouting voices joined the howling of the wind and the pounding of the waves: "Namu dai bosa, Namu dai bosa." I had no choice but to join him, although I felt great resistance. It seemed almost crazy, yet even so, I realized it was full of *nen*, full of intensive Mind.

Soen Roshi had been chanting the mantra "Namu dai bosa" ever since he created it as a young monk doing solitary retreats on Mount Dai Bosatsu. In the Nichiren tradition, they chant "Namu myo ho ren ge kyo"; in the Jodo Shin Shu (Pure Land) tradition they chant "Namu Amida Butsu." Soen Roshi often said that all sutras could be condensed into "Namu dai bosa," and that "Namu dai bosa" could be condensed into Mu, and Mu could be condensed into just sitting. With this kind of understanding, there is really no difference between "Namu myo ho ren ge kyo," "Namu Amida Butsu," and "Namu dai bosa." It is when we try to make literal distinctions that we miss the true meaning. In order to get that meaning, we have to drop our attachment to mental categories; then the true meaning can infuse us.

Soen Roshi tried to introduce this mantra into Japan, but the monks there resisted, thinking he wanted to become like Nichiren, founding a sect of his own. His American students, however, took it up readily. "The Japanese are not as sincere as the Americans," he said. "The Americans, not really knowing what the words mean, nevertheless have no problem with chanting them." Years later, after we established International Dai Bosatsu Zendo in upstate New York, he suggested that it would be an appropriate mantra for us.

For thirty-one years, on and off, I was with Soen Roshi, and as much as Nyogen Senzaki loved his teacher, Soyen Shaku, I loved my teacher, Soen Nakagawa. One of the great aspects of his teaching was his impromptu activation of the Dharma; another was that he did not overemphasize *kensho*; instead, he opened his students' eyes to the astonishing power of each moment.

One day we were riding in a car when all of a sudden he asked me, "Tai-san, what do you think about Ummon's 'Every day is a good day'?"

This is what I call spontaneous dokusan, unexpected dokusan; it could happen any time with him, which meant I had to be more with it, not only in the zendo but all the time, because I never knew when he would ask me something like this.

So while I was relaxing in the car he asked me, "What do you think about Ummon's 'Every day is a good day'?"

At first I said this and that; but the thing about him was that like a typical Japanese, he never said no directly. So when he didn't say anything, I knew it meant no.

Later on, still in the car, he asked me again, "How do you understand Ummon's 'Every day is a good day'?"

It happened to be March 5 that day, so without much conviction I simply said, "Today is March fifth." And he shook my hand. He didn't say anything like "Good," or "That's it." In human history we have never experienced today before, and we cannot repeat it. This is it. It's an unprecedented and unrepeatable day that we are living, and to fully understand it, to fully appreciate it, is the first step in Zen. To fully understand it is to comprehend Soen Roshi's definition of beauty. Now I might say, "Every day is a beautiful day."

On another occasion, he asked me, "Tai-san, what do you think about Nietzsche's 'God is dead'?"

This was so unexpected that I was speechless. So Soen Roshi answered, "God is not dead, since he was never born."

When I was Soen Roshi's attendant monk at Ryutaku-ji, there was an American professor who came to practice there. He was desperate to have some kind of insight experience. Evidently, the koan Mu had been assigned to him, without any kind of explanation.

Many months had passed and he was very frustrated. One day it happened that Soen Roshi invited him and me to his mother's hut to hear music and have ceremonial tea. Roshi said, "Be seated." We sat down. The professor's mind was occupied with the koan he had been assigned. He asked, "Tell me, Roshi, how can I expedite my understanding of Mu? What is the most effective way to practice Mu and get self-realization?"

Continuing to make the ceremonial tea, Soen Roshi asked him,

Soen Roshi at Ryutaku-ji

"What did Jesus Christ say on the cross?" The professor replied, "Well, he said, 'My God, my God, why have you forsaken me?'"

Soen Roshi said nothing and served the ceremonial tea, as if the conversation was over. But from the professor's point of view, it was not. So he asked again, "I came all the way from America; I want to know my true nature. So what is the most effective way to practice Mu?"

Roshi said, "Tell me, what did Jesus Christ say on the cross?" The professor replied again, rather impatiently, "'My God, my God, why have you forsaken me!'"

"No!" Roshi answered loudly. "Well, then, what *did* he say?" the professor asked in exasperation.

At that Soen Roshi stood up, spread his arms, became Jesus Christ, and cried in anguish, "My God, my God, why have you forsaken me?"

I was dumbfounded. The professor was too! No explanation was made. No instruction as such was given. This is the difference between explanation-Zen and becoming-Zen. Spontaneously, the true spirit of Zen Buddhism was expressed using a Western reference in an Eastern monastery, Ryutaku-ji, and in the English language. There was no East, no West, no Buddhism, no Christianity; the Way was dynamically yet subtly expressed.

Soen Roshi's mind rejected narrow categories like sectarianism and nationalism. His "Spiritual Interrelationship Day," as he wrote to Nyogen Senzaki, was for all "those who are interested in seeking the Dharma, wherever they reside on this planet." And just as the Venerable Senzaki hoped that an international language (Esperanto) might one day prevail, Soen Roshi wanted to create an international zendo. He was indeed a prophet of the Dharma. Although his efforts as a young monk in Japan to establish such a place were unsuccessful, many years later his dream came true when the Zen Studies Society, under my direction, bought fourteen hundred acres in upstate New York. Soen Roshi made his first visit to the property in the fall of 1971. One day we were walking together through what is now the Sangha Meadow, where departed Sangha members' ashes have been buried. We were talking about what to name the monastery, and because it is in the Catskill Mountains, we thought at first to name it Nansen Zendo (referring to the koan "Nansen Kills the Cat"). But that name somehow didn't seem right. We continued walking; we looked at the mountain, which seemed to have the shape of the Buddha lying on his side at his Parinirvana, and we thought perhaps that could be the name. After walking along a little further, suddenly it came into our minds simultaneously. International Dai Bosatsu Zendo! Soen Roshi was so happy. He said, "Finally, an international zendo!" He had had to give up that dream in his youth, but it became a reality forty years later in the United States. The Dai Bosatsu mandala was working its magic.

Soen Roshi loved this new Mount Dai Bosatsu and spent several weeks at a time there during the early stages of Dai Bosatsu Zendo's construction, living first in the original house on the property with a small group of resident students and then in the newly built monastery. He particularly loved swimming in the clear, cold waters of Beecher Lake. I once asked him why he liked to swim so much. "For two reasons," he answered. "For one thing, I like to be naked. For another, in the water I'm just an ordinary swimmer."

When he was in America, he could take off his "Japanese robes" and swim, as it were, among the American students, who, fortunately or unfortunately as the case may be, had no preconceived notions about monastic tradition and no awareness of the sort of social hierarchy one finds in Japan. Maintaining his public role in Japan took a great toll. Life there meant adhering to narrow social codes, always conforming to others' expectations. Being physically naked symbolized for him the ideal and natural state of the mind: free from any kind of acquired conditioning.

Soen Roshi enjoyed his visits to the United States, but he had no intention of remaining here. He once told me, "I love this country—as long as I don't have to stay more than three months." What he meant was that while he loved the plain, openhearted directness of his American students, sometimes their casual, rough behavior and naïveté offended his refined sensibility. The cultural differences between East and West grew too pronounced. After all, Japan was his home. He loved the delicate

Soen Roshi doing calligraphy

subtleties and sophistication of Japanese culture, particularly the Zen arts such as tea ceremony, Noh theater, and shakuhachi flute. Even though his English was quite good, he felt his poetic gift could be better expressed in his native tongue.

He also felt acutely the responsibility of maintaining and protecting Ryutaku-ji. In the late 1960s, for several years, Soen Roshi was involved in a fundraising project to purchase the land surrounding the monastery, where developers wanted to build a residential housing tract. Because of his shyness, it was very painful for him to ask for donations, even for an extremely good cause. It was also difficult because he was not accustomed to dealing with economic matters. And as usual with such projects, there were some people at Ryutaku-ji who disagreed with the need to expand the grounds. Soen Roshi found himself caught between his wish to protect the monastery with what he proposed to call "The National Teacher's (Hakuin's) Forest," and the sentiments of those who disagreed with the project; between being a public figure in order to raise money, and being a man of a very private disposition.

His yearning for solitude and respite from the pressures of fundraising may have led to the accident that occurred in September 1967 and changed his life. One day, he disappeared. At first, his attendant thought he had gone to Tokyo, which was something he would occasionally do alone. The attendant called all the places where he thought Soen Roshi might be, but he could not locate him. The following day, the monks went to homes and temples throughout the entire region, asking if anyone had seen Soen Roshi. They continued doing this the next day as well. "Not knowing how near the truth is, we seek it far away," as Hakuin says. They looked everywhere to no avail. Before reporting his absence to the police, they decided to search the monastery grounds. One monk, not expecting anything, stepped into a bamboo grove near the monastery, and there, among the sharp spears of bamboo, he found Soen Roshi, unconscious. Evidently he had climbed into the tree that grew just above this grove. Nobody knows how long he had been in the tree or on the ground. Nobody knows what he was thinking. And nobody knows why he even climbed into a tree instead of sitting on the zazen cushion, although he often spoke admiringly of the Chinese master Dorin, known as Bird's Nest Roshi for his custom of doing zazen in a tree. But my guess is that he climbed that tree to get away from all those conflicting pressures.

Soen Roshi was immediately taken to the hospital. The doctor said that if he had been found half a day later, he would have died. From what I understood, a piece of bamboo had pierced his brain. He was taken from one hospital to another during a period of several months and underwent many medical tests. The doctors advised an operation, although they warned it would be very risky. Soen Roshi refused, and he was never without pain from that time on. It was then that he began drinking a lot, to help dull the pain.

Soen Roshi had a close relationship with his sister-in-law, Chiyo Nakagawa, and she took care of him during his stay in the hospital. One day, while he was half asleep, she heard him speaking to himself: "What a stupid thing I did!" Later she asked him, "Brother, what did you mean when you said, 'What a stupid thing I did'?" He replied, "I will tell you later."

In America, on a day when he was in a good mood, I asked him, "Why did you climb that tree?"

He said, "I will tell you later." And then he added, "Truly, I will tell you before my death." I believed this and didn't ask again until 1982, when we were in Los Angeles together, staying at Hotel New Ohtani. Somehow I thought it would be a good chance to ask again. He replied, "I'm not about to die, so I'll tell you later." In fact that meeting was the last time we were together. He died two years later, and nobody ever found out what he meant when he said, "What a stupid thing I did."

Of course it is impossible to know for sure, but perhaps what happened was he got up in that tree and, looking out at the broad vista and seeing how far around the temple buildings the property extended, realized Ryutaku-ji really did have enough land. If he hadn't been embroiled in the fundraising, which went against his nature so terribly, perhaps he would not have climbed that tree. Soen Roshi might still be with us today, and the history of Zen Buddhism in America would be completely different.

This accident and his subsequent pain became his cross to bear, ceaselessly. Most of us do not wish anyone to suffer, whether physically, spiritually, or emotionally, and we will do whatever we can to help relieve such suffering. However, Soen Roshi's accident, ordinarily viewed as negative or unfortunate, can be seen as part of the Dai Bosatsu mandala. From this point of view it was necessary. Soen Roshi often said that we are all being danced, and that he was one of the dancers of pain. His suffering encouraged others who faced great suffering to continue and to become emancipated through self-realization.

After his lengthy hospitalization, Soen Roshi knew his health was not stable; he became worried about the future of Ryutaku-ji. He really loved being the abbot but felt he needed more rest and fewer responsibilities. His dilemma was when to step down. It happened much earlier than everybody expected. After many sleepless nights, he decided to appoint Sochu Suzuki to be the next abbot of Ryutaku-ji. From the midst of a one-hundred-day retreat, he wrote to me in February 1973: "This is the first letter I am writing since January first. I want you to know that I have made a decision to install Sochu as the abbot of Ryutaku-ji. It will take place on June third this year. I hope you can come for that installation ceremony. . . . Actually giving birth is far easier than this worry, worry, worry. After June, I can be emancipated from the abbot position, and then I can be a midwife for the birth of International Dai Bosatsu Zendo."

Of course, his way of being "a midwife" was not what I had in mind.

Soen Roshi often said that it was his chanting of "Namu dai bosa" on his solitary retreats in Japan that was responsible for International Dai Bosatsu Zendo's coming into being. I looked at it from another perspective. When I was building Dai Bosatsu Zendo in the remote Catskill Mountains of New York, I found that my monastery training had not prepared me to deal with labor unions, banks, prime rates, the gasoline shortage, architects, or fundraising. All of these skills I had to learn in a foreign country, in a foreign language. There were times when I was quite overwhelmed and almost gave up. If not for many worldly wise bodhisattvas, particularly the late William Johnstone, whose practical advice supported me every day, Dai Bosatsu Zendo perhaps could not have been constructed.

When Soen Roshi attributed its success to cosmic forces that he had set in motion, it seemed an irritatingly romantic view. I felt he ignored the muddy, painful world of dust and avoided getting his hands dirty with the hard work. He seemed to hold

Soen Roshi and Eido Roshi

himself aloof from such matters, often asking his students to take care of practical affairs.

However, while writing this introduction, something caused me to change my view. I spent many hours reading through all of Soen Roshi's letters to Nyogen Senzaki. They were written with a brush, like calligraphy on scrolls, and some were many yards long. A frequent theme in these letters was the significance of "Dai Bosatsu Mandala Day."

I was reading through a letter of 1938 written at Shinkyo, which

Spiritual Interrelationship mandala, from Soen Roshi's
letter to Nyogen Senzaki, 1938

was then the capital of Manchuria. In this letter, which unfurls
to more than thirty-four feet in length, I came upon a mandala
that he painted, similar to what one would find in the esoteric
Buddhist schools. Inside the outer circle, he drew a mountain.
Above the mountain is another circle with a monk sitting in the
center like Vairocana Buddha. In the middle is the character
Shinkyo and at the bottom he wrote "Los Angeles" and "ko rei
zu," "the diagram of spiritual interrelationship." At the top he
put the names of places important to him, such as Iwakuni, his
family home; Enzan, where Kogaku-ji is located; Gangyo-ji,
where he lived while he was at the university and where quite
often the monthly Dai Bosatsu evenings took place; the First
Academy Zendo, and two other places. The significance of all
these locations is described in detail in the letter.

I had read this letter several times over the years, but this time
something caught my eye that I had never seen before. To my
astonishment, I noticed a place name on the mandala: "Nakano,
Arai." When I read this, I shivered. The small district of Nakano,
Arai, in Tokyo, is where I was born. When Soen Roshi wrote that

letter, I was a six-year-old boy, living with my family in Nakano. I was recovering from a broken leg caused by an automobile accident. It was Nakano, Arai, where I first heard the *Heart Sutra*, at a Shingon temple, and where I had my first taste of the Dharma. Of course Soen Roshi and I had never met, and at that time I did not know anything about a Dai Bosatsu mandala.

Now, more than half a century later and on another continent, I find myself in the midst of this Dai Bosatsu mandala. Though I may never know why he wrote Nakano, Arai, on the top of the mandala, or what significance it had for him, it seems that I am part of the Dai Bosatsu mandala and cannot escape from it. So our chanting of "Namu dai bosa" is meant to be for past, present, and future generations—whether they know it or not.

I must confess that since reading this letter, I have had to rethink my criticism of his mystical claims for founding the monastery in the Catskills with the chanting of "Namu dai bosa." I now realize that his actions cannot be understood from the ordinary, rational viewpoint. Soen Roshi must be perceived from the vista of the cosmos, where the collective unconscious and the everyday world are not separate, and where the nonrational universe is continually manifesting itself in worldly events through what I call "Dharma arrangements."

It was a summer evening at Dai Bosatsu Zendo when I told my students about my discovery regarding Soen Roshi's letter and mandala; afterward we began chanting the names of our Dharma lineage. Suddenly, thunder and lightning began. Balls of hail rained down so hard on the zendo deck that it became pitted with small holes.

Now I can truly say that my mind is pacified. For more than thirty years, I have tried to escape from my karma like a shrimp trying to jump out of a net. The harder I have tried, the more I have failed. Disappointment and frustration always followed. I now know that just as the sun cannot leave the universe, I cannot leave this Dai Bosatsu mandala. And so I am grateful to my karma, to Soen Roshi, and to my students and friends. This is the reason I said, "The more the years pass the more alive he seems."

I just looked outside at the twenty-year-old roof, beautifully aged and covered with moss. It is indeed beautiful, and yet when I have regarded it in the past, I have not been able to keep from thinking about how we must replace it before the leaks start and how much it will cost and how we should raise the funds. But now, having recognized this Dai Bosatsu mandala for what it is, I feel completely different. If it is meant to continue, if it is necessary, the Dharma will arrange for the roof to be replaced. If it is not necessary it will not happen. I will not worry about the roof. There is only one thing that we all have to do, and that is to continue and continue doing *kessei*, sesshin, daily zazen, Namu dai bosa, Namu dai bosa. That's it! This is what I mean by pacification.

When Soen Roshi stepped down as abbot, he assumed that he would be treated as an honored master; when Gempo Roshi retired, Soen Roshi had always asked him to give teisho, and the ones from that period of time on the *Gateless Gate* are among the great masterpieces of Zen commentary. However, when Soen Roshi transferred power he soon felt out of place and unwanted. His mood swings and health worsened. When he retired he told me, "At last I am free," but I sensed sadness and loneliness beneath his words. One day when I was visiting Japan toward the end of Soen Roshi's life, someone told me, "Tai-san, Soen Roshi is so eager to see you." When I arrived at Ryutaku-ji, I went to see Sochu Roshi first, and he said sarcastically, "He is again in 'private retreat.'" When I went to see Soen Roshi, he said, "It is so painful I cannot even come to attend morning service." Whether he meant his physical and emotional condition, or whether he meant Sochu Roshi did not want him to attend, I could not tell. I went to Sochu Roshi and told him what Soen Roshi had said, and Sochu Roshi said sharply, with some degree of frustration, "If he wants to, why doesn't he come down?" He interpreted what Soen Roshi had said as a complaint, but I realized that Soen Roshi was simply saying that he was in such pain—whether emotional, physical, or psychological, or all of those—that he was unable to attend.

His accident was really a turning point in his life. Little by little he became a person of unpredictable, erratic behavior. Prac-

Soen Roshi going to Chichibu on pilgrimage, dressed
in a traditional monk's takuhatsu attire, 1977

titioners in America loved his spontaneity and viewed his actions as indications of his "crazy wisdom," but in Japan, people were not so understanding. Every now and then he would disappear into his room, saying he was going into *okomori*, a private retreat. Some of these retreats would last for a hundred days or more.

It was clear to those of us who knew him well that he was suffering from depression during the last few years of his life, but his need for privacy, his shyness, and his pride wouldn't allow him to admit it. His American students would have done anything for him, but he kept his pain hidden. He was an excellent actor; he enjoyed making up his own plays and participating in theatrical events. Even when he was depressed, in front of a visitor he could immediately seem engaging and happy, creating a merry atmosphere. He was so talented at that, but when his visitor left, his depression would come right back. So guests would say how fine he was; he would have given them an impeccable performance. I once asked him, "Don't you think it's unfair to do that?" He replied, "Why? They came to see me, and I gave them a wonderful time." Temporarily he would be better, but then he would be even worse; it seemed that the exhaustion from putting on such a good performance would leave him feeling lower than ever. It was a tragedy that he was so successful at covering up his depression. Indeed, he himself seemed to be deceived. After a while, he was unaware how much he was acting. Acting the role became natural. He acted a role with me as well, but after so many years with him, I could tell when he was performing. I tried to cover up for him, to protect him, because he refused help. I didn't want to invade his privacy.

I often thought, if only he had some good friend with whom he could speak openly. Despite our close relationship, I was too young, and after all, I was his student. I thought perhaps he could talk intimately with Koun Yamada Roshi, Yasutani Roshi's Dharma heir. Soen Roshi had been at school with him and had introduced him to Zen, but he could not open his heart. I think he suffered far more than we can imagine. Even aside from the neurological illness caused by his accident, being an abbot cuts one off. It's a position of great loneliness for many of us, and for him, due to his reclusive nature, his feelings of isolation were especially deep and intense.

In 1975, the officials at Myoshin-ji invited him to do the *rekiju kaido* (the one-day honorary-abbot ceremony, which implied the possibility of becoming the head abbot of Myoshin-ji some day). In Japan, to have elevated standing in the Rinzai Zen hierarchy, it was almost mandatory to accept this great honor. However, it involved taking part in a ridiculously expensive ceremony. He declined; it was the first time anyone had ever refused such an honor. I truly admire his bravery in pursuing his own truth, regardless of whether the establishment approved or disapproved. The frivolous conversation and gossip of others meant nothing compared to his realization of the quintessence of Buddha Dharma.

The excuse he made to Myoshin-ji was, "I will do rekiju kaido at Dai Bosatsu Zendo in New York." The Myoshin-ji authorities could not say or do anything. We had planned to install Soen Roshi as abbot of Dai Bosatsu Zendo at the formal opening ceremonies on July 4, 1976, but he never appeared. Knowing he was to be the principal guest, he had asked Sochu Roshi and another of his Dharma successors, Kozen Fujimori Roshi, to be the secondary guests, and he was sending many Ryutaku-ji monks as well. We had scheduled International Sesshin for the week leading up to July 4. On the day the Ryutaku-ji group was to leave Japan, Soen Roshi said, "Just go without me; I'll come later." When they arrived and told me, I thought he would somehow show up on the eve of the ceremony, or even that morning. I remembered that on the occasion of the opening ceremony for the New York Zendo on September 15, 1968, he had asked me to make arrangements to pick him up at the apartment of one of the senior students so he could make a dramatic entrance when everyone was seated and calm. The other roshis had been quite annoyed. After the ceremony he had secluded himself on the third floor. When I had asked him to come for a group photograph, he had refused. To my disappointment, that historic picture was never taken.

On the morning of July 4, 1976, we all waited, hoping he would arrive, but he never showed up. I thought he would be so thrilled to be part of this momentous occasion. I can only guess at his motivation for not coming. It could have been his illness, or his shyness about being the principal honored guest; it could have been to make a dramatic point through his absence. I was so eager to give Dai Bosatsu Zendo to him, but by not attending he gave it back to me.

Soen Roshi always said he admired "plain, natural, and direct behavior," but he was such a complicated, indirect, convoluted person. Once when I needed his help, I asked him to come to New York. He was doing okomori alone in his room and refused, saying, "Someone has to do this kind of practice." At the time, I didn't get it. I felt he was letting me down, and I was disappointed and resentful of his seemingly uncooperative attitude. From the cosmic perspective of the mandala, of course he was right. Someone had to do that kind of practice. Now I understand. It has been thirty years since he told me that. The Zen saying "Practice thirty more years" is not an exaggeration.

Soen Nakagawa Roshi passed away on March 11, 1984. He would have been seventy-seven years old on March 19. A birthday celebration was being planned at Ryutaku-ji, which he knew about. On March 11, he was visited by a haiku poet, Sumita Ohyama. They had a good time together, talking about haiku and drinking a lot. His guest left late, and he was alone; evidently he continued drinking, and around midnight he went to the bathhouse. No one was around; he got into the bathtub, and he may have fallen asleep in the warm water. The following morning a monk found him; he had drowned. Ironically, the same thing happened to Sochu Roshi some years later: after sesshin he went to a hot spring. No one was around; he got into the tub, had a heart attack, and died.

It was also ironic how I found out about Soen Roshi's death. Despite Soen Roshi's reservations, Sochu Roshi had scheduled his own rekiju kaido at Myoshin-ji, and he had asked me to come. Several weeks went by while I debated whether or not I would go.

It was March 11, 1984, when I called to tell Ryutaku-ji to say I would attend. Sochu Roshi immediately came to the telephone and cried out, "Soen Roshi just passed away!"

I flew to Japan immediately. A month later I returned for the official funeral service that was held at Ryutaku-ji. His ashes were divided into three parts: one third were buried with the abbots of Ryutaku-ji, one third went to the Nakagawa family, and one third I brought back to Dai Bosatsu. On July 4, 1984, we held a ceremony where I mixed his ashes with Nyogen Senzaki's ashes. A stone stupa has been built for these two founders of Dai Bosatsu Zendo: one half of the monument reads, "Mitta Kutsu Soen Zenji" and the other side says, "Choro An Nyogen Zenji." They are separated yet one. At International Dai Bosatsu Zendo, we uphold their tradition of bowing to each other on the twenty-first day of the month; we continue to celebrate Dai Bosatsu Mandala Day. Time after time, nature joins our chanting with thunder followed by bursts of sunlight, snow showers, and rainbows, and I cannot help but feel that these two pioneers of Zen Buddhism in the West are delighted.

Soen Roshi's nen was so strong! My karmic bond with him is such that regardless of human emotions, it cannot be separated. It is an everlasting, intermingled bond.

Daito Kokushi, the founder of Daitoku-ji in Kyoto, once said:

Parted from each other for millions of eons
Yet not even a second separated.

What Daito Kokushi meant in this verse was that our phenomenal self and our real self cannot be separated. My relationship with Soen Roshi is that close.

It has been more than twelve years since Soen Nakagawa Roshi's passing. If I were to choose one Zen verse for my late master, I would offer this particular one. It is here that the ultimate unity between him and me can be found. It is in this verse that one finds the everlasting teacher-student relationship.

October 1, 1995
International Dai Bosatsu Zendo
Beecher Lake, New York

Mandala Day Ceremony at the Stupa for Soen Roshi and Nyogen Senzaki,
July 21, 1993

PART ONE
ASCETIC PRACTICE
1931–1949

Enso

A young wanderer who is exhausting himself on the great matter of birth and death visits Meibaku hut, where I have secluded myself, on the night of the full moon, March 10. Although he and I have never met before, we immediately feel a strong bond, and we talk all night.

> Extraordinary link
> we find each other again
> bright moon

> Shōen no mata musuba re te tsuki akaki
> 勝縁の又結ばれて月明き

The next morning the sky and the ground are thick with snow. Our hearts leaping ahead of us, my new friend and I leave on a walking pilgrimage toward Tokyo, through Dai Bosatsu Pass. All beings are soundless, and the contours of the mountain ridges vanish into heaven's eternal breath. At the pass, deep with snow and illuminated by the moon, my friend experiences kensho, the liberation of seeing into his true nature. We yell back and forth to each other, holding hands and tumbling in the snow like madmen.

> Gratitude!
> tears melting into
> mountain snow

> Arigata ya namida ni tokasu yama no yuki
> ありがたや泪に融かす山の雪

On March 19, 1931, my twenty-fourth birthday, Keigaku Katsube Roshi shaves my head.

Gazing
with half-closed eyes
wintry spring

Hangan ni misukasu haru no mada samuki
半眼に見すかす春のまだ寒き

A monk's determination:

Clearness!
sky and water
reflecting my heart

Suzushisa ya kokoro wo utsusu mizu to sora
涼しさや心をうつす水と空

JULY 20, 1931

Upon vowing to eat only nuts, seeds, and raw vegetables:

Coolness
mouthful of melon
taste!

Suzushisa ya mankō fukumu uri no aji
涼しさや満口ふくむ瓜の味

NOVEMBER 3, 1931

On October 3, I made a vow to live on one meal a day, following
the teachings of early Buddhist scriptures. This has resulted in a
new-day clarity and expansiveness in my life. Now I realize that
eating white rice is not healthy, and I am changing to brown rice
and using only brown sugar.

Vast solitude
my thinning body
transparent autumn

Ryōryōto aki wa sumiyuku mi no hosori
寥々と秋は澄みゆく身のほそり

AUTUMN 1931

Since making that vow, I have been experiencing the joy of practicing it. One evening I hear a Zen teacher tell in his lecture about
eating forty-nine sweet rice cakes at a time when he was young. I
am appalled. But on my way back, I stop at a bakery and buy one
of those cakes. It is like the initial gunshot breaking the silence.
It creates explosive desire. One calls for another, and another. I
become so angry, even while devouring this unhealthy food, that
I feel like a demon.

> Bodily desire
> viciously raging
> this barren night

> Mi no yoku no mazamaza sugoki yosamu kana
> 身の慾のまざまざ凄き夜寒かな

AUTUMN 1931

There is a woman who has been grieving over me since I shaved
my head and left the householder's life. Her soul has grown thin,
as has her body. One hazy-moon night while living on this
mountain, I happen upon three dolls with rather unusual faces.
Although they appear lovely, innocent, and pure, behind their
faces lurks some mysterious spirit. I send them to the young
woman as a beautiful and melancholy memento.

> In these dolls' dreams of their youth
> two shells tossed by the waves
> touch each other softly,
> making a clicking sound.

> In these dolls' dreams of their old age
> the road is shining with particles of sand,
> and they wander about
> as monks.

AUTUMN 1931

I go to Kokurozaki to become a student of the haiku master Dakotsu Iida. Upon my return, I find that a Zen friend, in despair
over his terminal illness, has hanged himself.

"No ignorance, no end to ignorance . . ."

In the midst of
this boundless autumn
a hanged body

Chūkū ni sumikiru aki no mukuro kana
中空に澄み切る秋の骸かな

WINTER 1931

On top of Mount Temmoku I see a monk doing zazen with
death-defying determination:

Out in the blizzard
a monk sits
life and death matter

Kaze fui te sō ikishini no yukiakari
風吹いて僧生き死にの雪明り

AUTUMN 1932

Even with the slightest effort to crush and overcome delusion and
laziness, an indescribably vast and magnificent world emerges at
our feet. An ordinary person immediately becomes the master of
the three worlds, hero of the entire universe. But unfortunately
there are few who understand this.

How solemn
each patch of grass
illumined by the moon

Mottaina ya kusamura gotoni teru tsukiyo
もつたいなやくさむらごとに照る月夜

SEPTEMBER 1932

In August Choji, an ascetic, and I leave on a journey to search for gold dust at the northernmost border of Sakhalin Island. We hope to use the gold for a spiritual reformation project.

Life turns so real
heading further north
monk in autumn

Inochi hishito satemo kita yuku aki no sō
命ひしとさても北ゆく秋の僧

AUTUMN 1932

After studying about gold mine registration at the Sakhalin government office, Choji and I go to Toyohara train station, intending to stay there overnight. But unlike mainland Japan, here the waiting room is closed after business hours. They do not allow people to stay. So we walk to a city park and sleep there, wet with dew.

With all our stuff
kicked out of the station
chilly night

Nigurumi ni eki wo oware shi yosamu kana
荷ぐるみに驛を追はれし夜寒かな

AUTUMN 1932

The famous Bassui, founder of Kogaku-ji where I was ordained, appears to me and scolds: "You have engaged in worldly affairs, writing poems and talking about secular matters. You are self-indulgent and are going against monastery regulations. In what place shall I chain you?" I respond, "Roshi . . ." and he says, "Yes?" I remain silent. He lets me go.

Having entered the monastery
I now know
my life is less than a dewdrop

Tera ni ki te tsuyu yori chiisaki hito nari shi
寺に來て露より小さき人なりし

MAY 5, 1933

At noon the great white halo of the sun appears. The world is
illumined by this auspicious sign. The mountain village is celebrating Boys' Day, with carp banners large and small flapping
fiercely in the wind. I have heard that when our sincere wish is
perceived by the heavens, a white rainbow pierces the moon.
When I finish reciting the six hundred volumes of the *Avatam-
saka-sutra* on top of Mount Fuji, I witness such a white rainbow
thrusting toward the sun above the vast ocean of clouds. Ecstatic
with the solemn power of life, I have a vision: a buddha image
stands in a stone niche in front of me, his hands joined together.
I understand it to be the embodiment of the Great Bodhisattva
of Splendid Affinity, who brings all sentient beings to enlightenment. With great reverence, I invite the bodhisattva to join and
guide the painter Murashima and me on our pilgrimage to
Mount Dai Bosatsu.

Splendid affinity
sun's great halo
green leaves

Shōen ni hi mo ōgasa no aoba kana
勝縁に日も大暈の青葉かな

MAY 1933

It may be dusk; it may be dawn, judging by the dim light floating
on the distant horizon. A field of withered grass occupies my
entire view. The light is as soft as a yellow fox's fur. Two women
in black robes walk gently toward the horizon, guarding a young
girl whose hair hangs down in a shiny black braid.

Ancient Buddha Mind

I was in my freshman year at First Academy [in Tokyo] and was in agony, looking for something to which I could dedicate my life. I thought whatever I would do would be wasteful and meaningless, until I found an essential plan for my life. In my search for something absolute, the accumulated things of ordinary life seemed to be stupidly squirming about; they faded away one after another. Exhausted by a feeling of vacancy, I wept with sadness on the second floor of the dormitory.

One day in the corner of the dark library I accidentally opened a book by Schopenhauer, which revived me beyond comprehension. My seeking mind suddenly stopped, all the struggles disappeared, and a clear understanding was revealed in a familiar way, as if it were a memory.

Three years passed. In my freshman year in the literature department at Tokyo University, I went on a spring pilgrimage in Ise. I was staying at a Zen temple near Daigen Peak, and was planning to travel over the mountain pass the next day to visit Nara, the land of the ancient buddhas, which I had been longing to see for many years. That night, I dreamed of the black-robed women and the girl who were walking in the field of withered grasses. The two nuns took turns telling me the story of the young girl. She was on her way to be sold to someone in a far land. They wept while recounting the details of her life.

"How old is she?" I asked, with a sense of concern. "Five," one responded. "She's going to be sold anyway, so please show her great love as a farewell gift."

I picked her up and held her, with her delicate, round cheeks and her moonlit eyes. Embraced by a deep, deep green fantasy, I melted into the warm life of this girl. I was caught up in a swirl of love. The nuns were weeping and sobbing, but the girl's face seemed eternally serene.

While climbing on the path through Daigen Pass the next morning, I sometimes looked back at the ridges of the mountains in Ise. In the bright morning light, I felt submerged in the phantasms of the previous night's dream. The mystical image of the girl shone in the deep green light. With tears welling up, I climbed in an ecstatic trance.

The sun shifted suddenly. I woke up from this reverie. In front of me was a five-story stupa rising into the sky, where a threadlike crescent moon floated as if a remnant of my dream. I reached the top of the pass.

Three years later, through the meshing of various university experiences with periodic bouts of depression, I threw myself onto the path of monkhood. My soul gleamed at my having taken this great turning.

One day, I was wandering along the snow-covered path of Dai Bosatsu Pass, which is surrounded by high peaks: Fuji, Yari, Hodaka, Jizo, Shaka, and Shirane. The sky was clear and the snow on the ground around me was a glittering halo.

Waves of light shimmered and swirled; they splashed over me and boiled up around me. This vast brightness engulfed me and then subsided. Again it gushed up, overflowing, soaring, and dancing. Then it narrowed to one concentrated brilliant form. Ah! The white-robed Kannon Bodhisattva! I kept prostrating myself to this luminous image.

This was the same figure I had seen in the afterimage following my dream of the girl. While traversing the snow-covered pass, the boundary between dreaming and waking, between fantasy and reality was eliminated. Now I know that what I saw was Kannon Bodhisattva in the form of a young girl. How sad that she was going to be sold! What suffering she must have experienced in her human form. Such a story can only be described in a novel.

JUNE 20, 1933
[From the preface to *Shigan* (Coffin of Poems)]
I have accumulated tens of thousands of sheets of scrap paper, all covered with my poetic writings, articles, and journal entries. I keep them in a plain wooden box—a coffin—in a corner of my room. I realized that this coffin could become an attachment to someone like myself, whose intention is to wander freely in a life of nonhindrance. I started organizing these materials, planning to turn the full coffin into a pile of ash. But as a consequence, I

have compiled the first part of this anthology, and I now present it to those who have some Dharma connection with me.

AUTUMN 1933

On the day of the autumn equinox, the *Shigan* manuscript is completed. I visit Basho's hut in Sekiguchidai-cho [Tokyo] and dedicate the anthology to the image of Master Basho.

> These trashy poems
> I respectfully offer
> to the Other Shore

> Tatematsuru utakuzu nagara higan kana
> たてまつる詩屑ながら彼岸かな

AUTUMN 1933

> *Funeral Procession of a Prostitute*

> Subtle scent lingers
> on the casket
> tiny chrysanthemums

> Honoka nao aki wa kogiku no hitsugi kana
> 仄香なほ秋は小菊の柩かな

AUTUMN 1933

Master Dakotsu often says that horse chestnuts have a quality similar to Zen monks' heads. I place seven horse chestnuts he gave me on my desk, and staring at them I forget about the length of the autumn evening.

> Horse chestnuts
> like monks' heads.
> In my solitude
> I play delightedly with them
> while the night deepens.

Matter of great urgency
a nut rolls away
alive

Suwa koto zo konomi ikite wa koroge keri
驚破事ぞ木の實生きてはころげけり

MARCH 1934

I lead fifteen members of the First Academy zazenkai on foot
from Tokyo to Kogaku Monastery for sesshin. Wearing the caps
of the elite high school's uniform, walking in straw sandals and
laced leg coverings, and holding green bamboo canes, the students are filled with youthful vitality. Step by step we purify Tama
Canal, the viaduct for the city of Tokyo, and ascend Mount Dai
Bosatsu, which is still covered with snow, and which is itself a
source for the water in the canal. We all rejoice in our courageous
bodhi-seeking pilgrimage. The great sesshin at Kogaku Monastery, with Mount Dai Bosatsu in front of us and Mount Fuji at
our backs, includes solid sittings, earnest, intense dokusan, and
Dharma combat. It summons forth gallons of blood and tears.
The painter Murashima has also joined our pilgrimage and creates a long horizontal scroll depicting our Dai Bosatsu practice.

Splendid affinity
tenfold, twentyfold
plum blossoms

Shōen no toe hatae naru ume no haru
勝縁の十重二十重なる梅の春

APRIL 1934

Four of us, including haiku master Dakotsu, try to climb to the
top of Mount Dai Bosatsu. It is a complete failure. All we get is a
bunch of amusing episodes.

Negative effects
auspicious in the end
mountain spring

Gyakuen mo tsuini medetaki yama no haru
逆縁もつひにめでたき山の春

SUMMER 1934

Fasting Comes to an End

Flesh withering
among myriad petals
I stand alone

Niku kare te banda no hana ni tatazumi nu
肉枯れて萬朶の花に佇みぬ

SUMMER 1934

While secluded in a mountain hut, I live on offerings from nearby
farmers.

Tears of gratitude
biting into a cucumber—
Dharma flavor

Tada namida itadaku uri no nori no aji
たゞ涙いたゞく瓜の法の味

SUMMER 1934

At Mount Dai Bosatsu

Bupposo birds
about to sing
moon's bright light

Buppōsō naku beki tsuki no akarusa yo
佛法僧鳴くべき月の明るさよ

[From "Ten Haiku of My Choice," 1973]
I wrote that poem during a retreat deep in the forest at Mount Dai Bosatsu in Kai Prefecture, north of Mount Fuji in Japan, when I was twenty-five or twenty-six years old. The bright light of the moon filled boundless space that evening, and I knew the *bupposo* (Buddha-Dharma-Sangha) birds, a type of owl, were about to sing, as they did every night. Sometimes the bupposo birds would sing "bup-po-so" and somewhere else *hototogisu* [nightingales] would sing "kyo-kyo-kyo." I often heard this exchange of songs between the bupposo and hototogisu on the mountain.

At that time it was my youthful fantasy—an ambition that was really not an ambition—to construct a training center for producing great bodhisattvas on that Dai Bosatsu ridge. Originally Dai Bosatsu Mountain was regarded as a site for paying homage to the view of Mount Fuji. When one is climbing Mount Fuji one has no view of it. Nowadays Dai Bosatsu Mountain has become a place for hiking, but when I was there it was like the following haiku:

A monk living alone
maple leaves
cover the entire mountain

Sō hitori sumu manzan no momiji kana
僧ひとり住む満山のもみじかな

It so happened that the dream of building a training place on that Dai Bosatsu ridge came to fruition through the spontaneous activity of the Dharma, but not in Japan. It happened on sacred land deep in the Catskill Mountains of New York State, a place like Yamato Prefecture in ancient Japan, where deer visit and play. There is a clear lake called Beecher Lake surrounded by thousands of acres of national forest. It is an almost infinite wilderness and is a place where true Dharma friends can gather from all over the world, a place not limited just to Buddhism or Zen.

JANUARY 29, 1935
[First letter to Nyogen Senzaki, also addressed to Paul Reps]
Thank you very much for your unexpected letter from overseas
and the translation you sent me last December. In my mountain
hut, where I pass the time leisurely, I read your joint translation
of the *Gateless Gate* with great interest. I really appreciate your
effort in conveying this Great Matter. It is almost impossible to
translate Chinese texts into Japanese. How much more so to
translate them into English!

I have also just finished reading your translation of and introduction to *The Ten Ox-Herding Pictures* and I think it perfectly
conveys the spirit of "a transmission outside the scriptures." . . .

Mr. Reps's concern about the lack of calcium in my diet is
greatly appreciated. Although it is austere, my diet is nourishing.
While I eat only one meal a day, it is filled with delicious tastes,
and I am extremely grateful to nature for this bounty. It consists
of nine types of food: black beans, green beans, azuki beans, white
beans, soy beans, sesame seeds, pine nuts, pumpkin seeds, and
brown rice. While chewing these things one after the other, I mix
buckwheat powder with water. I also eat radishes, carrots, greens,
fruits, seaweed, and pine leaves—whatever is available. I don't
use fire; I eat everything raw. Recently I have stopped using salt,
unless it occurs naturally, as in seaweed. I take all things as they
come in nature. My excrement is small and has no smell. It just
rolls out like birds' droppings. Perhaps this is a kind of indul-
gence!

It has been said, "It is not that there is no Zen in Japan, but
that there is no Zen master." In the past I was repeatedly disappointed in my search for a true teacher, but recently I vowed to
practice to the death in the hall of Gempo Yamamoto Roshi.

Soon I will begin a pilgrimage around Shikoku with another
practitioner.

> Now turning toward
> the mustard flower path
> ringing a pilgrim's bell

> Iza saraba nanohana michi wo suzu no oto
> いざさらば菜の花道を鈴の音

SPRING 1935

Upon vowing to make a barefoot pilgrimage around the eighty-
eight temples of Shikoku:

> Straw sandals tossed aside
> approaching distant mountain slopes
> haze!

> Waraji sute yamasaka tōki kasumi kana
> 草鞋捨て山坂遠き霞かな

SPRING 1935

> Life or death
> together with the Buddha
> pilgrimage

> Ikishini wo hotoke to tomoni henro kana
> 生死をほとけと共に遍路かな

AUTUMN 1937
[First trip to Manchuria]
Arriving at the Korean port of Pusan:

> Autumn rain
> a random display
> souvenir shops

> Aki no ame komagoma narabu miyageten
> 秋の雨こまごまならぶ土産店

AUTUMN 1937

On board the superexpress train of the Continental Railroad, I
watch the Korean landscape passing by outside the window. Here
and there among the mountains and rivers serenely melding together, poplar trees stand like unfinished dreams. The low, scattered houses are encircled by nature. A man in a white robe

stands near a tree, a long, thin pipe in his mouth, watching the train go by.

> On a Korean highway
> one autumn day
> a traveler was walking.

> Wearing a white robe
> and a black-crowned hat
> he carried a sack over his shoulder
> and a long cane.

> Through the window
> of the speeding train
> by chance, to my surprise,
> our eyes met.

> It was a face
> I had seen
> a long, long time ago.

AUTUMN 1937

When I look out the window of the express train, hurtling through Korea toward Manchuria, I see a distant reddish-brown mountain on the horizon that looks like a flying dragon. I don't know its name, but it touches my heart. I soon arrive at the border station, where every article in my overstuffed monk's bag is taken out and examined by the customs official. The train is strictly guarded by soldiers; its windows have blackout curtains pulled down, to prevent it from being seen and attacked by bandits. In the depth of night, the train crosses the bridge over the broad Yalu River and roars into the plains of Manchuria.

> Eyes closed
> I hear the voice of autumn
> from the Shin dynasty

> Me tsumure ba Shin no yo kara no aki no koe
> 目つむれば清の世からの秋の聲

AUTUMN 1937

At the Myoshin-ji branch temple in Shinkyo, Manchuria, the schedule is: at three AM we wake up, have our washing ritual, go to morning service and zazen, clean the monastery, and study the ancient teachings. At 10:30 we have our first meal. Afterward there is a work period. At four PM we have evening service and zazen; at nine PM we retire.

One day after morning service, as usual I cross my legs in the lotus posture, place my hands together, elongate my spine, and make my Dharma body immovable. On this day I go into a dawn samadhi that is bright and clear. Nothing, not even Buddha Dharma, is in the way, let alone the wasteful delusions of the transmigration of birth-and-death! In this samadhi of samadhis, the lives of the ancestors enter my life; my life enters into theirs. Now I can touch upon the essence of an earlier Dharma dialogue I had with Gempo Roshi. I knocked on the door of his tiger's cave and went in to dokusan. I was scratched by the master's great compassionate claw, and I experienced my original before-birth childhood, ending that dawn practice glaring through my own tiger's eyes.

Not knowing
this is a gourd bush monastery
the moon shines down

Hyon no ki no tera tomo shira nu tsukiakari
瓢の木の寺とも知らぬ月明り

OCTOBER 3, 1937

I leave Shinkyo in September for mainland Japan, so that I can hold a memorial service for my father and visit a friend who is a patient in a psychiatric institution. On October 3, on the twentieth anniversary of my father's death, I prostrate my wandering monk's body in front of his tomb.

Samadhi

Entering autumn
mountains and rivers
winds blast forth

Aki ni iru yamakawa tomini kaze tachi nu
秋に入る山川とみに風立ちぬ

OCTOBER 7, 1937

On October 6 I visit Y. at the psychiatric institution in Ijima,
Shikoku. More than one hundred residents live here in noisy
chaos, isolated from the rest of the world. At eight AM the following day, after a medical checkup, inmates judged to be sufficiently
healthy are taken by guards through the iron gates to wade in the
ocean. About fifteen or sixteen mentally troubled men and
women take a dip in the water, then stand around shaking and
shivering. They walk to the stone *torii* gate of Awai Shrine and
back again, over and over. Under the bright autumn sun some
look sorrowful; others act like clowns. I join them for a while in
their jumping up and down.

Mad people
send up a cheer
gumi berries are red

Kyōja ra ga hayashi te gumi no irozuki nu
狂者らが囃して茱萸の色づきぬ

OCTOBER 8, 1937

Today Y. and I are given a room to ourselves. Four inmates with
various Buddhist backgrounds come to see us. Everyone does
brushwork on paper for Bodhidharma Day. Y. uses his masterful
hand to paint a magnificent image of the first ancestor of Zen
and signs his name. Since it was recently Bodhidharma Day [Oc-
tober 5], the topic of conversation turns to the ultimate point of
religion. They laugh and laugh.

Although the six sense organs of these friends are slightly
askew, these sense organs themselves are mere phantasms. Fun-

damentally, not a single thing is owned. Those of us who jump around in response to these mere phantasms and act according to right and wrong, gain and loss, self and other, and this and that, are we not mad as well?

I leave the institution on a steam passenger launch. Sitting half-naked in zazen on the roof of the cabin, I drum upon my hara until the boat disappears behind an island. People probably think I am one of the crazy ones.

> From high barred windows
> mad friends peek out
> autumn sea

> Takamado ya kyōja ga nozoku aki no umi
> 高窓や狂者が覗く秋の海

AUTUMN (OCT. 8?) 1937

> *Bowing to Hakuin's Stupa at Ryutaku-ji in Mishima*

> Endless is my vow
> under the azure sky
> boundless autumn

> Aozora ni waga gan tsuki zu aki tsuki zu
> 蒼穹にわが願盡きず秋盡きず

AUTUMN 1937

> May this maple leaf
> from Hakuin's stupa
> cross the ocean

> Hakuintō no momiji hitohira umi koe te
> 白隠塔の紅葉ひとひら海越えて

AUTUMN 1937
[Back in Manchuria]

Traveler's longing—
I place my palm on the ground
autumn wind

Akikaze ya daichi ni te wo oku tabigokoro
秋風や大地に掌をおく旅ごころ

AUTUMN 1937

A community of lamas
fast asleep
under the midnight sun

Ramatachi no neshizume te iru byakuya kana
喇嘛達の寝しづめてゐる白夜哉

WINTER 1937

In winter
the seven stars
walk upon a crystal forest

Nanatsuboshi juhyō no sora wo ariku naru
七ツ星樹氷の空を歩りくなる

[From "Ten Haiku of My Choice," 1973]
I wrote that poem in Manchuria, before World War II. It was a
night in which the vast steppes were completely encased in snow
and ice. I was traveling on foot, following the North Star. The Big
Dipper was in the sky above the forest; every tree was blooming
with flowers of ice. My walking and that of the stars became one.
About that time I also wrote the following poem:

My urine turns to
cloud mountains
on the ground

Haya ute ba tachi narabi tari kumo no mine
はやうてば立ち並びたり雲のみね

This may seem strange, but it reminds me of another poem, a
favorite of mine:

Aiming my penis
out over the steppes
awoken from a nap

Ochinko wo kōya ni sue te hirunezame
おちんこを曠野に据えて晝寝覺め

The word *penis* had never been used before in haiku, and I was
criticized for exposing such a thing! But a penis is just a penis.
Nowadays there is confusion regarding sex. But in truth, sexual
energy, like digestive energy, is God's fine energy, Buddha's energy, cosmic energy.

SPRING 1938

Fifteenth Day of Fasting

Mirage of flowers
for my sacred meal
wraith body

Seisan ya yūtai ni shi te ayagasumi
聖餐や幽體にして彩霞

MAY 1938

Looking for serenity
you have come
to the monastery.

Looking for serenity
I am leaving
the monastery.

Kwatz!

Stop running about seeking!

The dusty affairs of the world
fill the day,
fill the night.

SUMMER 1938
[Another trip to Manchuria]
Deep at night I had a dip in a hot spring, surrounded by the vast
plains. I looked up at the constellations; the stars were dancing
in the field of the sky. I was totally absorbed in "this Matter" and
vowed to settle in a hut on Mount Dai Bosatsu.

Distant thunder
various races naked
in the stone tub

Enrai ni izoku mutsume ru yutsubo kana
遠雷に異族睦める湯壷かな

SUMMER 1938
Going down the Amur River in a steam-driven paddlewheel boat,
I am able to do a lot of zazen. The great river running through
the broad open vista permeates my soul day by day. At midnight
I cross my legs on the prow of the upper deck.

Beneath the dome of stars
the prow of this boat
sets its course

Manten no hoshi ni senshu no sadamari nu
満天の星に船首のさだまりぬ

Celestial Dance

AUTUMN 1938

Autumn day
waves crash
glittering copper

Aki no hi no akagane no gotoku nami uchi nu
秋の日の銅の如波打ちぬ

AUTUMN 1938
[Letter to Nyogen Senzaki]
I hear that the tension along the Soviet border is increasing. In
the past there was no draft for Japanese citizens in the area, but
nowadays people are frequently being drafted for the military. I
have no intention of holding a gun and shooting Chinese gentle-
men. But there may be some things to do in some nonaggressive
way, such as consoling people, so I don't mind if I am drafted.
On the occasion of a military assault I would be rolling around
on the ground with the wounded soldiers. Battlefields must be
chaotic places, so I'm sure there would be a lot of straightening
up to do.

I am staying at a farm near Shinkyo, but I will visit the branch
temple of Myoshin-ji soon and will caress the tiger's whiskers. I'd
like to be excused from wasteful time in the monastery, so I will
be camping out at a friend's place. Gempo Roshi is planning to
go back to Japan at the end of this year. Since he is quite old, I
would like to attend him as much as possible while he is here.
Although I am determined to seclude myself in the mountains as
we discussed, I will be in Shinkyo until the old master returns to
Japan.

AUTUMN 1938

At Nachi Falls

Under the clear autumn sky
my bow extends from the ocean
to the mountain waterfall

Akibare ya umi kara ogamu yama no taki
秋晴や海から拝む山の瀧

AUTUMN 1938

[Letter to Nyogen Senzaki]

I have been studying your teisho on the *Gateless Gate* one after another. I feel emancipated just seeing the teaching conveyed in Roman letters rather than ideograms. Zen, which is fundamentally about the emancipation of all beings, is unfortunately sealed in some square box called Zen. In this enclosure the ancient dog in the koan "Joshu's Mu" has been suffocating. In English this "dog" is so joyfully alive!

> In an empty house
> autumn is ending
> Noh chanting

> Kūkan ni aki mo hate naru utai kana
> 空館に秋も果なる謡ひ哉

WINTER 1938

> *On the Occasion of the Death of Inindo Sensei*

> One note of the shakuhachi
> resounds endlessly
> piercing the winter clouds

> Fuyugumo no tōtoki kagiri kakure keri
> 冬雲のたふときかぎり隠れけり

WINTER 1938

> Icicles surround my hut
> massing day after day
> an ice fortress

> An meguru tsurara ukara to nari ni keri
> 庵めぐる氷柱族となりにけり

WINTER 1938

Shivering through a shallow sleep
in this night of extreme cold
dawn at last

Gokkan no asaki nemuri ni ariake nu
極寒の浅き眠りに有明ぬ

WINTER 1938

A nun has come to visit
now in the moonlight
how bright the icicles!

Ama mo ki te tsurarazukiyo to nari ni keri
尼も來て氷柱月夜となりにけり

APRIL 1939

Disappearing
snow on mountain peak
unfurls a rainbow

Kiegate ni mineyuki niji wo hiraki keri
消えがてに嶺雪虹を開きけり

SPRING 1939

Soft spring rain—
since when
have I been called a monk?

Haru shigure itsu yori sō to yoba re ken
春しぐれいつより僧と呼ばれけむ

SPRING 1939

I came to this mountain
looking for enlightenment.
There was no enlightenment
on the mountain.
Whether laughing or crying
all I hear is an echo
from the other side of the mountain.

SUMMER 1939

Again in Seclusion on Mount Dai Bosatsu

Great peak!
knowing where to go
ants in single file

Ōmine ya yukue wo shitte ari no retsu
大嶺や行方を知つて蟻の列

SUMMER 1939

Deep autumn
among the rocks
trees bend in one direction

Iwa no kigi mina aki fukaki katanabiki
岩の樹々皆秋深き片なびき

SUMMER 1939

Raking
fallen leaves
stillness permeates the mountain

Manzan no shizukesa ochiba kaki ni keri
満山のしづけさ落葉掻きにけり

NOVEMBER 1939

[Letter to Nyogen Senzaki]

The other day, Gempo Roshi held his zazenkai at the Hakusan Dojo in Koishikawa, Tokyo, so I went to Tokyo for the first time in a long time and saw him.

At the zazenkai, the owner of an eel restaurant who had rescued an antique sculpture of a mountain ascetic from a pawn shop asked me to bring it to my mountain hut and enshrine it.

On the night before I first met Gempo Roshi, I had a dream of an ascetic wearing a persimmon-colored, short-sleeved robe, walking briskly through a broad field. While I was in Manchuria with Roshi, at one point he looked exactly like the ascetic in my dream. Roshi often says that he was an ascetic who broke the precepts in a former life, and therefore he was born nearly blind in this lifetime. This sculpture of a mountain monk's face and posture remind me very much of Gempo Roshi. Indeed, when I showed him the sculpture, he said, "This must be me in a former life."

CIRCA 1939

[Letter to Nyogen Senzaki]

Every month, on the twenty-first day, at eight PM local time, let all Dharma seekers on the planet join in spiritual communication. Will you be good enough to chant "The Great Compassionate Dharani" [which begins "Namu kara tan no"] at that time? I will ask my shakuhachi friends to join me in my "Namu kara tan no" chanting.

SPRING 1943

During the War in the Pacific

News of a victorious battle
I just shuffle along in the mud
at this spring temple

Senka tada tera no shundei fumu bakari
戰果たゞ寺の春泥ふむばかり

SPRING 1944

> News of a disastrous battle
> I just shuffle along in the mud
> at this spring temple

> Senka tada tera no shundei fumu bakari
> 戦禍たゞ寺の春泥ふむばかり

1944
Looking up and seeing a large formation of B-29s for the first time:

Air Raid

> Earth, water, fire, and air—
> bombing these four elements;
> form, feeling, thought, volition, and consciousness—
> annihilating these five skandhas.
> Sitting here
> I hear a roar in winter's blue sky.

> Five . . . six . . . planes go overhead
> then
> five . . . six . . .
> one.

> Sparkling stars
> in the daytime
> darting
> like eyes.
> Those who fly the planes
> are light-haired strangers.
> The flashes, the blasts,
> the explosions
> come closer.
> Ah!
> An air raid on my "self."

MARCH 10, 1945

In commemoration of the multitudes killed in the massive air raid over Tokyo:

Early spring
spirits
spark up into emptiness

Ryōshō no hinoko hitonoko mina kū ni
料峭の火の子人の子みな空に

WINTER 1945

Rebirth

Having survived the fire, leafless trees
shiver under the dawn sky.

A couple with a child
pass through
burdened by unbearable anxiety about the day.

Monks with begging bowls appear—

Five monks, six,
another group of five, seven,
one—

Flapping ink-black sleeves
stepping silently in straw sandals
absorbed in thought
gazing far beyond.

Those who give are empty
those who receive are empty
offerings themselves are empty.

Step by step they practice
these three empty circles.

Chanting Ho [Dharma]
Ho
Ho.

Thus the voice of Dharma
fills the devastated city
from one end to the other.
All insects under the ground
are awakened
all seeds nod to each other,

And
the capital,
which disappeared like a dream,
will again
be born like a dream.

So set forth the Prajnaparamita mantra.
Set forth this mantra and say,
Ga-te Ga-te! Para ga-te!
Parasamga-te! Bodhi! Svaha!
Prajnaparamita Sutra.

JANUARY 1946

City of ash
Fuji soars serene
New Year's first light

Yakeato ni Fuji shizumari shi hatsuakari
燒あとに富士しづまりし初明り

SPRING 1946

A mother and son
in the monastery bath
moon above plum blossoms

Tera no yu ni haha to ko ga ori umetsukiyo
寺の湯に母と子がをり梅月夜

SPRING 1946

New-formed plum
new-formed dew
each born to the other

Ume no mi no ko to tsuyu no ko to umare au
梅の實の子と露の子と生まれ合ふ

APRIL 8, 1946

Today Father Maxima has completed his great sacred mural, *The
Birth of Buddha*. While secluded in Saint Nicholas Cathedral in
Tokyo, even throughout the air raids, he painted with every
ounce of his being. To celebrate the completion of the mural, a
bunch of artists get together. We have a great time chanting sutras, playing shakuhachi, and having tea ceremony until late at
night. Even some American people join us, arriving in a jeep.
Friends and enemies: one blossoming dream.

All beings are flowers
blooming
in a flowering universe

Hana no yo no hana no yō naru hito bakari
花の世の花のやうなる人ばかり

Buddha (Butsu)

JUNE 1946

Up all night listening
to the soundless flute
June

Minatsuki no fuka nu fue kiku yomosugara
水無月の吹かぬ笛聞く夜もすがら

DECEMBER 1946

During *rohatsu* sesshin [an eight-day retreat at the beginning of December commemorating Shakyamuni Buddha's Enlightenment] in the Great Doubt Zendo at Ryutaku-ji, reflecting on the Tokyo air raid:

Middle day of rohatsu
sitting with us
a GI

Beihei mo ki te nakabi naru rōhatsue
米兵も来て中日なる臘八會

SUMMER 1947

Great Doubt Zendo

Wheat ripens
whispering sound
circling

Mugi ururu oto hisohisoto mi no mawari
麥熟るる音ひそひそと身のまはり

SUMMER 1947

There is a thatched-roof hut on the mountain behind Ryutaku-ji. It has become a soul-nest for Mr. T., who is exhausted, having worked for the government since the end of the war. I named this hut Is That So, after an episode in Hakuin's life.

> Fragrance of lilies
> throughout the night
> dreaming for a nation

> Yuri no ka ni yo wa yomosugara kuni no yume
> 百合の香に夜は夜もすがら國の夢

SUMMER 1947

A former admiral comes to listen to Hakuin's "Sound of One Hand."

> Narrow miss as a war criminal
> now at rainy season
> visiting a temple

> Sempan ni more te aru hi wo tsuyudera ni
> 戰犯に洩れて或る日を梅雨寺に

SUMMER 1948

At Ryutaku-ji there is a practitioner who is half paralyzed. He cuts and splits firewood and carries water with one hand, and he is a master at stoking the stove to heat the bath water. He heats the water for me whenever I take a bath.

> Dripping sound
> never stops
> behind the monastery

> Shitatari no koe tsukuru naki tera no oku
> 滴りの聲盡くるなき寺の奥

SUMMER 1948

Sculptor G. is working in the storehouse of the monastery. Although he is quite slow in attaining buddhahood in the zendo, when he swings his chisel Shakyamuni and Bodhidharma appear one after another, just as he envisions them. Now a bunch of artists with long hair are getting together.

Carve the mandala
of the stars
on this ancient tree

Furuki ki no hoshimandara wo horiidase
古き樹の星まんだらを彫り出せ

JANUARY 1949
[Telegram to Nyogen Senzaki]
Entry permit to USA granted. Rest assured.

JANUARY 1949
[Letter to Nyogen Senzaki]
The great sesshin commemorating Buddha's enlightenment, rohatsu, was held this year from January 18 to the dawn of January 25. Under the ancient stupa of Hakuin, in the Great Doubt Zendo, twenty-five of us sat knee to knee. The billowing Dharma ocean grew calm in this period of eight days compressed into one. For the first time in a long time, I served as jikijitsu. Tears kept welling up in my eyes with the joy of interconnected life and the heartbeat of the true Dharma. In the land of joy and in the city of angels also there will be practitioners sitting like mountains facing the wall. Clappers are struck; the bell is rung; buddhas and bodhisattvas as numerous as the sand of the Ganges emerge from the ten directions.

In the United States and also in China, all we can do is conduct this great sesshin. This, I believe, is the essential of essentials. Zazen, kinhin, zazen, kinhin.

I hope you received my telegram that I was granted an entry permit to the United States. Now I need to go to the Ministry of Foreign Affairs to get my passport, and to the doctor for a physical examination. What would you advise about travel arrangements? Could you pick a convenient day at the beginning of

March? Any kind of cabin would be fine, since I can do zazen anywhere. Oh! to be sitting on the Pacific Ocean!

MARCH 1949

It was around 1875 or 1876. A woman's corpse was lying in a remote village in the Kamchatka Peninsula [Siberia], Russia. She had left behind a poem grieving about her fleeting life. A baby lay exhausted at her frozen breast, no longer able to cry. An itinerant monk approached from a huge cloud beyond the steppe, picked up the baby, wrapped him in his Dharma robe, and took him to Japan. Thus he was provided with a Dharma connection.

This orphan, of whom it was not known whether the father was Russian, Chinese, or Japanese, was raised by the family of a boat builder named Senzaki in Aomori Prefecture.

The young boy heard about the Messiah from a missionary who visited the village, but he felt a strong attraction to the Dharma, and when he was nineteen he read the entire Tripitaka. His sense of impermanence grew stronger, and he became a monk at the age of twenty-one. He studied with outstanding teachers in various schools of Buddhism, and finally the Dharma body of Nyogen was revealed under the strict guidance of Soyen Shaku Roshi, abbot of Engaku-ji. Nyogen accompanied Soyen Shaku Roshi to a new continent, the United States of America, and remained there for more than thirty years. Living among all types of people, he continued his practice with great patience. One day about ten years ago, I received a photograph of Master Nyogen, with his white hair and look of serene composure, from across the Pacific Ocean. The poem he sent along with the photograph read:

> One by one
> please come here
> under the moonlit window
> with a bowl of whisked tea
> for a koan

But at the time I was practicing austerity, living naked in the far reaches of Mount Dai Bosatsu, so a bowl of whisked tea seemed

Namu Tea

far from my world. Dozens of photographs and letters followed. Before I could send even a piece of a photograph of myself, the war started, and we could communicate only Mind to Mind. After the war was over, I sent to Los Angeles a photograph of thirteen Zen practitioners gathered around Gempo Roshi at Ryu-taku-ji. Jokingly I asked Master Nyogen to pick out my face from among these thirteen. He and members of his sangha pored over the photograph, trying to figure it out, and finally picked one face, offered tea to the photograph, and enjoyed a moment of the fragrant breeze. Then they wrote to me and told me whom they had picked. Their choice was correct. Mr. T., who happened to be visiting me, took a picture of me accepting a bowl of tea from the Phantasm, Nyogen. [Nyogen means "like a phantasm."] In this way, the ten-year-old koan of how to get to his moonlit window thousands of miles beyond the Pacific Ocean was penetrated. We made old times the present, and made the present the past; the day for visiting the United States was near at hand.

Spring approaches
the Pacific Ocean
will be my sitting mat

Haru chikashi Taiheiyō wo zabuton ni
春近し太平洋を座布團に

APRIL 1949
[United States]

Arriving at the Other Shore

The great round mirror of the boundless ocean
has disappeared in the dark blue night.

This boat is now speeding toward the east
at twenty-one knots per hour
at a north latitude of 130 degrees
bound for a country of science, for a country
of atomic bombs.

The *General Gordon* is a huge white dragon
chewing its way through the cresting waves
of eternal eons' samsara
and shooting seven-hued rainbows
across the dome of the sky.

Assembled on the deck are
a Jewish painter
a Canadian journalist
a Polish missionary
and a Japanese physicist.
All share a bowl of tea served by this wandering monk.

Do you or do you not know:
hidden in this bowl of tea is a secret
more secret than all of atomic science.

All things are born of interrelated conditions.
Therefore, not a thing has a separate identity.
Because there is no separate identity
this one bowl can contain even more than the Pacific Ocean.

Not coming
not going
not attaining
thus in the end empty.

In this way, even if I thoroughly penetrate into
the emptiness of the three billion great worlds
still there is more emptiness to fathom
and tomorrow morning I will arrive
at the other shore,
San Francisco.

SUMMER 1949

For Jimmy Tanahashi

Your slightest sorrow—
how dense the summer forest!—
my sorrow deepens

Kanashimi no awaki ga kanashi natsu kodachi
かなしみの淡きがかなし夏木立

DECEMBER 1949

Santa Claus
in a monk's black robe
receives my wild embrace

Sumizome no Santakurōsu ni dakitsuke ri
墨染めのサンタクロースに抱きつけり

DECEMBER 1949

Vast emptiness
as the year comes to a close
I re-enter the mountain

Kakunento toshi hatsuru hi ya yama ni iru
廓然と年果つる日や山に入る

PART TWO

EARLY YEARS AS ABBOT

1951–1959

One hand
waving endlessly
autumn ocean

Itsumademo furi shi sekishu ya aki no umi
いつまでも振りし隻手や秋の洋

Upon Daisetz Suzuki's departure, although I missed his airplane,
not knowing Summer Time [like Daylight Saving Time] was
over:

Corn is ripe
in the fields
approaching the airport

Kūkō no soba made kibi no ure te ori
空港のそばまで黍の熟れてをり

Mendicant descends
to the village
moonless night

Gyōkotsushi mugetsu no mura ni kudari keri
行乞士無月の村に下りけり

Acorn hits
my shoulder
just before dawn

Donguri no waga kata ni otsu yoakemae
團栗のわが肩におつ夜明前

WINTER 1951

In the chorus of snores
an American friend is also heard
this frosty night

Beijin no ibiki mo majiru shimoyo kana
米人の鼾もまじる霜夜かな

WINTER 1951

Coming out of the clouds
full moon freezes
over the monastery.

Kumo wo dete tera no mangetsu itetsuki nu
雲を出て寺の滿月凍てつきぬ

JULY 1952

During a visit from Paul Reps, a poet wandering through the
world, at Ryutaku-ji:

Traveler: Watch Out!

Oppressive cloud
we talk about
the atomic age

Kumo atsuku genshijidai wo katariau
雲暑く原子時代を語り合ふ

JULY 1952

Morning service
offering its fragrance
a white lily

Gongyō ya shirayuri asa no ka wo age te
勤行や白百合朝の香をあげて

JULY 1952

At last
I have met
my own cool star

Mizukara no suzushiki hoshi ni ai ni keri
自らの涼しき星に逢ひにけり

SEPTEMBER 1952

Drops of fresh dew
vow renewed
side by side

Mangan no suzushiki tsuyu wo narabe keri
満願の涼しき露を並べけり

Abundant persimmons
delivered to the monastery
sensuous glow

Kaki amata tera ni todoki te tsuyameki nu
柿あまた寺にとゞきて艶めきぬ

SEPTEMBER 1952

Among the corn stalks
wind rippling
just for the corn

Kibi no ha ni kibi no kaze dake kayou rashi
黍の葉に黍の風だけかよふらし

Sweeping the monastery yard
autumn's sound
deeper day by day

Tera hake ba hi ni hi ni fukashi aki no koe
寺掃けば日に日にふかし秋の聲

Into the twilight zendo
maple leaves
come dancing

Zendō no naka nimo mai nu yūmomiji
禪堂の中にも舞ひぬ夕もみじ

[From "Ten Haiku of My Choice," 1973]
In autumn, maple leaves from the mountain forests surrounding
Ryutaku-ji sailed in the wind, dancing. Some of them flew into
the serene zendo.

In the bath
with my aged mother
annual Day of Storms

Tarachine to yu ni iru nihyakutōka kana
タラチネト湯ニヰル二百十日哉

Stars drift down
aligning themselves
rohatsu sesshin

Hoshi hikuu ori te narabi nu rōhatsue
星低うおりてならびぬ臘八會

Into the twilight zendo—maple leaves—come dancing

DECEMBER 1952

End of the year
woodcutter walks through mud
steps on clouds

Toshi kikori nukarumi wo fumi kumo wo fumi
年木樵ぬかるみを踏み雲を踏み

[From "Ten Haiku of My Choice," 1973]
A woodcutter goes to a mountain to collect firewood for the New
Year. He sometimes walks through muddy spots on the path and
gets his feet dirty. He slips and falls into adversity, or he strides
on the clouds.

JANUARY 1953

Old mountain monastery
this New Year's Day
brightening

Shōgatsu mo furuku akaruku yama no tera
正月も舊くあかるく山の寺

SPRING 1953

Basking in the sun
my eighty-eight-year-old teacher
budding branch of plum

Ume fukumu hinata wo beiju rōtaishi
梅含む日向を米壽老大師

SPRING 1953

Spring shower
inconsolable
I get on a train

Haru shigure yaruse nakere ba kisha ni nori
春しぐれやるせなければ汽車に乗り

I remember a letter from Ryuta Iida, who is the son of my master Dakotsu and is himself a leading haiku poet in Japan. He told me he and another distinguished poet, Yasoku Ishiwara, expressed their appreciation for that "I get on a train" poem when they were at Shirahone Hot Spring.

If I were to pick a representative anthology of Basho's haiku, it would be perhaps *The Monkey's Raincoat.*

> First winter rain
> monkey, too, wishes for
> a small straw raincoat
> —Basho

A wonderful poem, isn't it? But no one would select such a poem if this were presented at a haiku meeting or a selection committee now.

SPRING 1953

> Picked
> by an old woman's hand
> herbs glow green

> Uba ga te ni tsuma re te kusa no moyuru nari
> 姥が手に摘まれて草の萌ゆるなり

[From "Ten Haiku of My Choice," 1973]
That poem represents a world where plus and minus are one. Kitaro Nishida's philosophy describes the self-identification of absolute contradiction. To be dying is to be living, and to be living is to be dying. Death and life cannot be separated. They only have different names.

When we talk about the spiritual realm, we may feel that it is a place where we go after we die. Most people think that we live in the actual world while we are alive, and that after we take the last breath we somehow wander into a vague realm of the spirit. It is a great mistake to see two separate realms. Instead, where we live is in fact the spiritual realm, a realm of many billion worlds, which goes beyond three, four, or even infinite dimensions. Then the danger is that we might think that this is a realm that is empty and boundless. Watch out! It's all manifested right here at this moment. It is alive and kicking!

We can't just sit there in the realm of absolute equality. At the same time that we experience a world where all is one, we see the world of differentiation, where not one thing is the same. The world of absolute differentiation is, as it is, a world of absolute equality.

Here an old woman, a grandmother, is picking some herbs. As soon as she picks them, new shoots come up.

I did not intend to create a haiku expressing the Zen viewpoint, but this is how things really are. We often hear the phrase in the *Heart Sutra,* "Form is emptiness, emptiness is form." It is not just that form is a tangible realm and emptiness is a spiritual realm. These realms are not two, but one. Even if you realize they are one, you can still get trapped by the idea of oneness.

The following poems express a similar feeling to the one about the old woman picking herbs:

> Wisteria blossoms
> fading
> *saha* world

> Fuji no hana ase tsutsu shaba no chimata kana
> 藤の花あせつゝ娑婆の巷かな

> An old bhikshuni
> with nothing to do
> sneezes

> Rōbiku no shiyōkoto mo naku hanahiri nu
> 老比丘のしやうこともなく噎りぬ

SPRING 1955

How interesting, that people in Japan continue to serve special treats while saying, "We have nothing." There's no better greeting in the world than this. Truly, from the beginning there is not a thing. This is the abundant feast. Let me offer this to you as a New Year's treat.

Encouraging Words

Step by step
a new-born lamb
eternal spring

Kohitsuji no ippo ippo ni towa no haru
小羊の一歩々々に永久の春

FEBRUARY 5, 1955

In the air from Tokyo to Los Angeles on February 5, the thirteenth day of the lunar calendar, on my second visit to the United States:

Disk of the sun, disk of the moon
together in the clouds
spring begins

Risshun no hi no wa tsuki no wa kumo no naka
立春の日の輪月の輪雲の中

SPRING 1955

In Los Angeles I hear there are two cars for every five people, and there is something called a freeway that goes in two separate directions, each with two or three lanes, with spiraling ramps. The drivers search for something called parking places. In the middle of this city, Japanese and American Buddhists establish a Zen hermitage, centering around old man Nyogen Senzaki. It seems Buddhism is still traveling eastward. I'm a guest here, a wondering wanderer, doing nothing.

Car after car
shining
in the spring breeze

Jidōsha no hitotsu hitotsu ni kaze hikaru
自動車のひとつひとつに風光る

MAY 1956
Telegram to Shuji Tanahashi, Shubin's husband, who returned to
Gifu, Japan, for the first time in forty-two years:

This is not a dream
the green leaf of a persimmon
after forty-two years

Yume nara zu shijūninen no kaki wakaba
夢ならず四十二年の柿若葉

JANUARY 1957
Sekiren has completed her vow to draw five hundred thousand
images of Jizo Bodhisattva and has decided to extend her vow to
one million.

Embraced by the golden wind
all things bear fruit
round and full

Kimpūri mono mina maruki mi wo musubu
金風裡ものみな丸き實をむすぶ

WINTER 1957
When I took a walk on the mountain path behind Ryutaku-ji
with a Zen student from France named Manuel C., we were
thrilled to have a clear view of Mount Fuji. We walked all the way
up to the top of Mount Hakone. Neither of us had a single thing
in our pockets or in our stomachs. We started to worry, and then

suddenly someone appeared. It was K., a priest from Atami. I was
so struck by meeting him there. He lent us a Dream Hall note [a
thousand-yen bill, with a picture of Prince Shotoku's meditation
hut], so we were able to return by bus.

> Mountain peak
> at the height of winter
> lucid serenity

> Santen no fuyu wo kiwame te uraraka ya
> 山顛の冬を極めて麗かや

SPRING 1957

Doing zazen with patients at the leprosy clinic on the twenty-fifth
day of every month:

> Nightingale sings
> this very place is
> the lotus land of purity

> Funyoki nai te tōsho sunawachi rengekoku
> 不如歸鳴いて當所即ち蓮華國

SPRING 1957

> Sound of mountain
> sound of ocean
> everywhere spring rain

> Yama no oto umi no oto mina haru shigure
> 山の音海の音みな春しぐれ

SUMMER 1957

> Dusk
> surrounds the zendo
> this year's young bamboo

> Zendō no gururi no yami no kotoshidake
> 禪堂のぐるりの闇のことし竹

SUMMER 1957

Mr. I. secludes himself in a hut behind Ryutaku-ji with a vow to practice his koto exercises one thousand times.

> Milky Way
> notes of the koto
> vow nearly fulfilled

> Amanokawa mangan semaru koto no oto
> 天の川満願迫る琴の音

JANUARY 1958

Bhikshu, bhikshuni, upasaka, and *upasika* [monks, nuns, laymen, and laywomen] are considered to be the four types of practitioners. Auspiciously, all of these kinds of Dharma friends are here, including Zen students from France and America. Purifying the six sense organs, all together we reach the top of Mount Fuji.

> There is no Buddha
> other than This:
> higher than Fuji
> cloud mountains
> gleaming.

JANUARY 1958

Human knowledge has come to the point where living beings can spin around outside the earth's orbit. If we do not turn the light toward true wisdom, we will go off the track and destroy ourselves. Does a dog have buddha nature or not? An ancient buddha said, "Mu!" Investigating this Mu, we celebrate the New Year with a wish for humanity's inexhaustibility.

> Buddha Mu Mu Mu Mu
> Buddha Mu Mu Mu Mu Mu Mu
> Buddha Mu Mu Mu Mu

> Mumumumumu mumumumumumumu mumumumumu
> 仏ムムム仏ムムムムムム仏ムムムム

Inexhaustibility

MAY 8, 1958

In the midst of dawn zazen on May 8, we receive a telephone call from Los Angeles that old man Nyogen [Senzaki], who stirred up a Zen wind in America for more than half a century, has passed away.

> Phantasm and phantasm
> walk together
> summer begins

> Maboroshi to maboroshi yuke ba natsu asaki
> 幻とまぼろしゆけば夏浅き

MAY 8, 1958
[Letter to Nyogen Senzaki]

This morning as usual we woke up at 3:30 AM. After morning service in the Dharma Hall, there were two dawn sittings. During the first sitting, I was in the zendo with the monks. Then the attendant monk hurried up to me and informed me of a telephone call from Los Angeles. At that very moment, as though struck by a bolt of lightning, my mind was joined by yours. I heard Sister Shubin's [Tanahashi] lamenting voice; Brother Bai-oh's clear "OK!" The faces of McCanenny-san and Seiko-san seemed visible to me.

> I am joining
> in your meeting
> with one mind!*

During the second sitting I called the monks to dokusan. The first one who came in was a young novice monk (nineteen years old) who joined the monastery early this April from the country-side of Shikoku Island. Although he just started zazen very recently, he has been getting into samadhi quickly and deeply. Completely filled with samadhi joy, he told me that though he

* Written in English.

hadn't slept for the past four nights and days, he felt as clear as ever.

What about before your birth?

What about after death?

Even these questions he answered clearly, one by one. Indeed, this must be the working of his karma, not only in this lifetime, but life after life.

The fourth person to come in was Monk Eido [Shimano], and his koan happened to be Tosotsu's "Three Barriers":

"If you realize your true nature, you are free from life and death. When your eyes are closed, how can you be free from life and death? If you are free from life and death, you will know where you are going. When the four elements are disintegrated, where will you go?"

On this occasion, at this time, we thoroughly examined and clarified this particular koan, as I believe this is the best way to express our gratitude to you.

After finishing dokusan, I went up to Gempo Roshi's quarters and informed him of your departure. He was lying on his bed but said, "He was a reincarnate, and will work even harder for the Dharma now that he is without hindrances."

I completely agree with him. Nyogen, Nyoho [Like a Phantasm, Like Dharma], please guide us on our path and in our practice with all your might. Please give us your encouragement in our pursuit of Buddha's incomparable Way.

At 6:00 AM, we took our breakfast. When you visited here in 1955 you sat at this very place and we ate rice with azuki beans to toast your safe return to the United States. Just as we did that time, with some twenty monks and serious lay students, we are dedicating ourselves to the Buddha's Way. Please rest assured.

After breakfast, I announced your departure to all the monks and lay students. Three of us, Manuel C. from France, Monk Eido, and I, offered incense and flowers (from my mother's hut) and we all listened to the lecture you had given at the Tuesday talk at the Los Angeles Zendo on September 19, 1952, which had been recorded by Sister Seiko. I was deeply moved by what you said about the Way of Renunciation.

Today I will go to Koyama Zenkai (a group of lepers who meet for Zen practice). After the evening *han* we will hold a memorial service for you, chanting "The Great Compassionate Dharani," and we will listen to your recorded voice ("Searching for the Treasure"). As I think more about our unthinkable karmic encounter during this lifetime, many scenes and images flow through my mind like a picture scroll. I was getting ready to send cherry blossoms to your bedside for comfort, but as usual, being a poor letter-writer, it turned out to be too late. However, now I feel it was all right. This Matter is beyond correspondence and beyond words and letters, and I have even come to think that in the final analysis, Mind alone is good enough.

Last night I was in Mishima for the Zen meeting (held every seventh day of the month). I asked my friend Mrs. Meio, who will soon perform the Noh dance "Tomoe," to sing a passage from it.

> Falling petals know it is fundamentally empty
> flowing water knows it has no fixed mind
> mind clears all by itself . . .

After that was over, I gave a talk on "Karma and Fundamental Emptiness." I assume your departure may have taken place just around that time [Japanese time, 9:00 PM May 7; Los Angeles time, 5:00 AM May 7].

MAY 26, 1958

Upon the departure of Manuel C., on his way back to France by ocean liner after completing a year and a half of life in the monks' hall:

> On the deck
> a thought of midnight sun
> I whisk a bowl of tea

> Kampan no byakuya ni nitaru ocha tachi nu
> 甲板の白夜に似たるお茶點ちぬ

JULY 1958

In an airplane on my way to a Zen hermitage called Tozen [Moving Eastward] in Los Angeles:

> Soaring through the sky
> for Day of the Deceased—
> vast America

> Ama kakeru dai Amerika no urabon'e
> 天翔る大アメリカの盂蘭盆會

SEPTEMBER 1958

The departure of the boat I was going to take back [from Los Angeles to Yokohama, Japan] has been delayed three days, until October 1. We moved Choro-an Zendo [Senzaki's meditation hall] to Shubin's house across the street. Nothing of the zendo is left.

> Autumn light
> fills the room
> vacancy

> Ippaini naru aki no hi ga garandō
> いつぱいになる秋の陽ががらんどう

OCTOBER 1, 1958

At five PM Dharma friends, both Japanese and American, assembled for a final period of zazen. Chanting "The Four Great Vows," we placed the urn with the ashes of Old Man Nyogen into a monk's traveling bag. Cars formed a procession to Wilmington Port [Los Angeles]. The disk of the evening sun was reflected up and down the freeway.

> Friends' faces
> reluctant to part
> golden wind

> Kimpū ni wakare tomo nashi tomo no kao
> 金風に別れともなし友の顔

OCTOBER 13, 1958

Buddhism first arrived in Japan on this day in the thirteenth year of Emperor Kimmei's reign, 552 CE. On this voyage I also brought thirty thousand images of Jizo Bodhisattva, from among the one million images of Jizo Bodhisattvas Sekiren has painted in fulfillment of her vow. I have been sending these bodhisattvas out over the water as the ship speeds toward the West. Meanwhile, three American Zen friends who left Los Angeles on October 7 on the boat after mine are now floating somewhere on the Pacific Ocean. Coming and going, coming and going, we are all It in the Dharma ocean of thusness. Now I make a bowl of tea.

All in one
outstretched sky, autumn water
celebration

Kotohogu ya chōten shūsui mina hitotsu
壽くや長天秋水みなひとつ

JANUARY 1959

The so-called twelve causes and effects, the transmigration of birth and death, all are originally pure and empty. How auspicious!

The twelve signs
renew a cycle
year of emptiness

Jūnishi no hitomeguri shi te kū no haru
十二支の一めぐりして空の春

JANUARY 1959

Fierce storm
in the midst of the storm
first sunrise of the year

Ōshike no shike no naka naru hatsuhinode
大時化の時化の中なる初日の出

PART THREE

TEACHING IN THE WEST

1959–1972

At midday I land in Anchorage, Alaska. Having left in the evening, I arrive at noon of the same day. If you take a jet, it is possible for you to arrive before you have left! Past and future are all cut off. "Today is the eighth of the month, and tomorrow is the thirteenth." "Fish swim in the trees, and birds fly in the ocean." Such statements by old Zen teachers cannot be appreciated enough.

Flying through the clouds
white night
Alaska!

Arasuka no kumo tobi tsukusu byakuya kana
アラスカの雲飛びつくす白夜かな

After flying for nine hours I arrive in Honolulu. The first sesshin in Hawaii is held from February 3 to 8. People from different countries and of various races enter samadhi, in one hall, with one mind. Right after we arise, during *kinhin* beneath the star-filled sky, the breeze swirls through the palm leaves, cooling our feet. Behind the dojo, among the steep, ragged-edged rocks, tall cactus plants stand in groups like humans. Cardinals sing their high-pitched tunes in harmony with white-eyes [a species of bird imported from Japan that has proliferated in Hawaii] and pheasants. These birds manifest a paradise. "Water, birds, trees chant Buddha's name, chant Buddha's teachings." When I asked the name of the mountain that spits out the great disk of the sun each morning, I was told, Mount Koko. In the native language, Koko means blood-red as seen in a rainbow. Splendid! Each shower brings a seven-hued masterpiece that seems raised by the mountain's gentle curve. So I have named this new zendo Koko-an (koko hut), in resonance with "This very place *(koko)* is the lotus land," from Hakuin's "Song of Zazen."

Each tropical blossom
everlasting world
of everlasting summer

Tokonatsu no tokoyo no hana no hitotsu zutsu
常夏の常世の花のひとつづゝ

SPRING 1961

At the age of ninety-six, Gempo Roshi is still vital. He has probably signed his name "Hannya" [*prajna,* or wisdom] more than
eighty-four thousand times. The poetic theme given by the emperor to this year happens to be "youthfulness." I am celebrating
the true body that is before birth and beyond old age by whisking
tea in a bowl on whose inner surface Gempo Roshi wrote "youthfulness," and on whose exterior he wrote "old age."

Young ox
plodding home
original spring

Wakaushi no ayumi ayumi te moto no haru
若牛の歩み歩みて元の春

AUTUMN 1961

The preparation of a monastery for winter may seem unremark-
able. Everything that needs to be attended to is done, yet no trace
of effort is apparent. This expresses the spirit of my teacher,
Gempo Yamamoto Roshi, who spent most of his time doing
zazen, and who was often completely absorbed in studying the
Diamond Sutra. He would say that you are not yet mature if you
are seen as great or wise by others. It is not good to be absent-
minded, but you should be unpretentious while being aware of
all necessary matters. This is important!

Zen monastery
unpretentiously prepared
for winter

Zen'in no akkerakan to fuyujitaku
禪院のあつけらかんと冬支度

Prajna (Hannya)

JANUARY 1962

This is the Year of the Tiger, a creature of great daring. It is said that tigers make journeys of one thousand miles, returning in one day. We live in a time of emergency; even the earth's atmosphere is polluted. Yet there is a realm that is originally pure; not even a speck of dust can alight there. Returning to the original source, let us be as swift as tigers on this path!

> Great earth
> not even a lick of mud
> year's first laughter

> Daichi tsuchi hitoname mo nashi hatsuwarai
> 大地土ひとなめもなし初笑

AUTUMN 1962

> Into the same hut
> sun and moon enter
> autumn wind

> Ichian ni hi mo tsuki mo iru aki no kaze
> 一庵に日も月も入る秋の風

SPRING 1963

Under the bodhi tree in Bodhgaya, I burn again the remains of my teacher and my mother and offer the *Heart Sutra* of the entire heaven and entire earth to them.

> Moon, humans
> just as they are—
> bodhi spring

> Tsuki mo hito mo bodai no haru no sono mamma
> 月も人もボダイの春のそのまんま

SPRING 1963

India—
your sun has penetrated
even into my heart

Kokoro nimo Indo no hiyake ichijirushi
心にもインドの日燒けいちじるし

SPRING 1963

Baptising Myself in the Jordan River

Veiling the sound of
the murky water
young leaves shoot forth

Sasanigoru mizuoto hime te konome fuku
さゝ濁る水音祕めて木の芽吹く

SPRING 1963

A Bodhisattva assembly has just formed in Jerusalem. I am nam-
ing it the Dead Sea Sangha at Mount O-Live.
   Today I have bathed *on* the Dead Sea; now I may die!*

Crawling out of the Dead Sea
body glittering
with drops of spring†

Shikai yori haiide te haru no mi no shizuku
死海より這出でゝ春の身の雫

[From "Ten Haiku of My Choice," 1973]
You may know that the Dead Sea lies on the lowest part of the
earth. For millions and billions of years the density of the water

* *Written in English.*
† *Translated by Soen Nakagawa.*

has increased, because the water from the Jordan River runs into it but does not leave it.

It's called Dead Sea in the Western world because no bacteria or fish can live in it. But to us, it is filled with mysterious life beyond description. Different types of medicines and cosmetics are made from this water.

It's impossible to swim in the Dead Sea, since everything floats there. I once sat on the water with a few friends and had a tea ceremony. One fantasy I have is to invite political leaders from Israel and the Arab countries for tea there. At any rate, I managed to creep out of the sea and saw my entire body glittering with drops of water.

There is a hall for zazen on top of a hill covered with olive trees in Jerusalem. It is interesting that a Zen dojo is in this sacred city for Jews, Christians, and Moslems. If you go out onto the roof of the zendo in the morning, you can see the huge sun emerge from the Dead Sea beyond the desert of Judas. You do kinhin on the roof, and when the direction of your walking changes, you face the olive hills. You see "o-live" and "dead" from the same place. I made a keisaku out of an olive tree there. If I hit your shoulder with it, life and death in one vibrate throughout the world. This is not an exaggeration. If something happens in Moscow it is transmitted over televisions and radios instantly. How much more so with the waves of spiritual energy!

SPRING 1963

In Vienna

Leftover snow
dark day in the city
unbroken thread of music

Zansetsu no kuraki miyako ni gaku hitosuji
殘雪の暗き都に樂ひとすじ

APRIL 1963

After observing the full-moon ceremony with Buddhist friends in London on April 8, Buddha's birthday, I went to Copenhagen and then flew over the Arctic Circle on my way back to Tokyo. While I was away a great number of people helped create a prajna waterway—an underground plumbing system—at Ryutaku-ji.

> After a long journey
> hooting owl
> rush of water

> Tsuku naku ya kaeritsui taru mizu no oto

SEPTEMBER 1964

I traveled around the globe, picking up pebbles from all the different countries and placing them in one bag. Now I swing it around, contemplating the sound.

> Touching one another
> each becomes
> a pebble of the world

> Fureae ba dore mo sekai no koishi kana

SEPTEMBER 1964

Mr. Z. dedicated himself to creating two hundred white porcelain tea bowls. On the inside, he put Gempo Roshi's last calligraphy, the character *gen* [profundity], and offered the bowls to Roshi's students and close friends. Mr. Z. named the bowls Celebration of Life. This "life" does not refer to long duration, but to the experience of our own true face, which has no birth and no death. Day by day and night after night, it turns the vibrant wheel of the Tathagata endlessly. As I write this haiku there is a water shortage in Tokyo and the water has been turned off.

In the midst of the dry city
I whisk a bowl of tea
refreshed!

Ichinaka no kakute sawayaka ocha wo tatsu
市中のかくて爽やかお茶を點つ

JANUARY 1965

This is already the fortieth year of the Showa era. On the first day
of the Year of the Serpent, with the two hundredth anniversary
of Hakuin Zenji coming up in two years, we celebrate the actualization of the truth: "Sentient beings are primarily all buddhas
. . . This very body is the body of the Buddha."

Year of the Serpent
already uncoiling
self itself

Haru wa mi no sudeni hodoke te onore kana
春は巳の已にほどけて己かな

JULY 1965

It is said that *Bon* (the Day of the Dead), or *Urabon,* which came
from *ullambana* in Sanskrit, means being hung upside down.
How can we bring about freedom from such suffering?

Within this torment
wonderful coolness
moon of the Bon

Kurushisa mo sonomama suzushi bon no tsuki
くるしさもそのまゝすゞし盆の月

AUGUST 17, 1965
The Staff

There was a foolish servant whose master said to him, "This is a
staff for the most foolish person in the world. Find someone

more foolish than yourself and then give it to him or her. Until then, always keep it with you."

The servant took the staff. Feeling mortified, he looked for someone more foolish than himself but could not find such a person. Meanwhile, the master became gravely ill and was near death. He was bound for a destination far, far away.

The fool asked, "Where are you going?"

"I don't know," the master answered.

"What route are you taking?"

"I don't know that either."

"Are you all packed?"

"Not a bit."

Slapping his knee, the fool yelled, "You're leaving for a long journey and you don't know where you are going, you don't know how you're getting there, and you aren't ready to go? Indeed, you are the greatest fool in the world." The servant gave the staff to his master.

We all have such a staff, even though it is invisible. Thanks to this staff, this world is enjoyable, and the next world is enjoyable. It is said, "Someone who does not know is Buddha."

SEPTEMBER 1966

It's a time of potential crisis. The neighborhood surrounding the monastery will be made into a residential apartment area if we don't do something about it. We at Ryutaku-ji are in the process of expanding the monastery grounds, planting pine, cedar, and cypress trees. This will be called the National Teacher's (Hakuin's) Forest and will provide a deep Zen practice place for future generations. Just think: someone like Hakuin, or even half the measure of Hakuin, may be born here in five hundred years, or one thousand years. Such a person will increase the radiance of the Buddha's sunlight and will continue turning the Dharma wheel. We, too, will be at play in this forest, forging ahead on the unsurpassable path, birth after birth, generation after generation.

A monk
in real estate—
as shaky as raw tofu!

Tochi burōkā to nari tsutsu sō no hiyayakko
土地ブローカーとなりつゝ僧の冷奴

JANUARY 1967
Buddha Dharma has perished in India; Zen has declined in China; it has maintained its life vein in just a few scattered areas of East Asia. Now it is crossing the Pacific Ocean, moving eastward to the United States and going westward to Europe and Africa, and is about to blossom. This year is the two hundredth anniversary of Zen master Hakuin's death, and it follows the eleven hundredth anniversary of Rinzai's. Bodhidharma says one flower opens five petals. Thinking of how the true Dharma prevails on the five continents, as well as in our five inner organs, I am overcome with tears, and bow. This year, as I celebrate the calendar's return to the Year of the Sheep—my sixtieth birthday—I pray for an auspicious future for all beings.

Returning
and returning
ancestral teachers' spring

Tachikaeri tachikaeri tsutsu soshi no haru
たち返りたち返りつゝ祖師の春

SPRING 1968
Not seeing the maple leaves, not noticing the autumn moon, my mind blank and dark for one hundred and thirty days.

Big headache
small headache
spring keeps on jumping

Ōzutsū kozutsū haru no mai shikiru
大頭痛小頭痛春の舞ひしきる

SPRING 1968

Grave illness—
a lone mountain
smiles

Shibyō e te hitori emi iru yama mo ari
死病得てひとり笑みゐる山もあり

SPRING 1968

Driving along with monks Kozen and Sochu and some other Zen
friends on our way to Kai [Yamanashi] Prefecture, we stop at
Gekko-ji. We unexpectedly encounter a Buddha image engaged
in one-pointed concentration: an insect, vibrating its wings with
its entire mind and entire spirit, as transparent as a spinning top.

In midair
a horsefly hovers
young leaves shoot forth

Chūkū ni abu todomari te konome nobu
中空に虻とゞまりて木の芽伸ぶ

JULY 7, 1968

Above my floating belly
lover-stars meet
for just one night

Ukimi shi te tanabataboshi wo hara no ue
浮身して七夕星を腹の上

JULY 1968

I am visiting the United States for the sixth time. With me on
board ship is an image of the Tathagata of Infinite Light [Ami-
tabha Buddha], which has long stood on the main altar at Ryu-

taku-ji. Kazuki [Sekida] is in Honolulu, Sochu in London, Dokyu in Jerusalem. They are sowing the seeds of zazen practice, true Dharma, and universal peace, in an effort to liberate all beings from suffering.

> Coolness in mountain temple
> Dharma net now spread
> East and West
>
> Yama suzushi hōmō ima ya nishi higashi
> 山涼し法網今や西ひがし

SEPTEMBER 15, 1968

True Dharma abides endlessly; conditions are ripe. With the intense and passionate vow of the young monk Eido Tai Shimano, the New York Zendo Shobo-ji is born in Manhattan. The weather is gorgeous—Bodhisattva weather. Is it an autumn day in the Nara period, or a day at the time of Shakyamuni?

> Cleared-up
> sky of Japan
> now in America!
>
> Amerika no nippombare to nari ni keri
> アメリカの日本晴れとなりにけり
>
> Like a day
> of an ancient autumn
> today's New York
>
> Furuaki no aru hi no gotoshi Nyūyōku
> 古る秋のある日のごとしニューヨーク

AUTUMN 1968

> I scoop up
> the invisible footsteps of my teacher
> under the lofty sky
>
> Ten takaku shi no ashiato wo hiroi keri
> 天高く師の足あとを拾ひけり

Cleared-up—sky of Japan—now in America!

Vow fulfilled
I enter the disk of the sun
this autumn day

Mangan no aki nichirin ni ayumi iru
滿願の秋日輪に歩み入る

AUTUMN 1968

Awaiting
a teacher of humans and devas
moon and stars

Machi nozomu ninten no shi ya hoshizukiyo
待ち望む人天の師や星月夜

JULY 1969

Master Kyogen said, "A man is up a tree, holding onto a branch
by his teeth, with his hands and feet in the air, and he is asked,
'What is the meaning of Bodhidharma coming from India?'
[What is the ultimate meaning of liberation?] How would you
respond?" Modern civilization is often topsy-turvy in its approach to life, including matters of clothing, food, and housing.
We need to return to a natural way of life. Traffic calamities are
rampant and pollution is intensifying; this earth, together with
the three billion realms of beings, may explode from nuclear
weapons. At this point, what is the ultimate meaning of liberation?

Now, Now, It's the Day of My Ceremony for the Dead

Into the universe
of transparent stillness
hands and feet splatter

Suzushisa no sora ni chiru nari te mo ashi mo
涼しさの宙に散るなり手も足も

SEPTEMBER 1969

The first day of the first month of 5729 in the Jewish calendar corresponds to the middle day of Higan in Japan (the day of crossing over to the Other Shore). It is also the day of a full solar eclipse. In this mysterious light, Jerusalem's bodhisattva assembly, called the Dead Sea Sangha, has formed at Mount O-Live Kibutsu-ji [Founding Buddha Temple, a play on the word *kibbutz*].

> Sky high
> a young child rides
> on a young donkey
>
> Ten takaku kodomo no roba ni kodomo noru
> 天高くこどもの驢馬に子供乗る

SEPTEMBER 1969

> Bodhisattva Ridge
> moon expanding
> over Jerusalem
>
> Bosatsune ni tsuki futoru nari Erusaremu
> ぼさつ嶺に月太るなりエルサレム

[From "Ten Haiku of My Choice," 1973]
It is not that there is a mountain called Bodhisattva in Jerusalem. In fact Mount Bodhisattva, which actually has the shape of a bodhisattva, lies on the banks of Beecher Lake in upstate New York. So I could have put "New York" instead of "Jerusalem." But the idea is that the moon on the ridge, the moon of the bodhisattva is waxing and spreading its light. Don't you think "Jerusalem" provides a rather powerful sound, image, and texture for this poem?

JANUARY 1970

Shakyamuni Buddha was born in the flower garden of Lumbini at the foot of the Tree of No Anxiety. He attained great enlightenment at seeing a star through the blossoms of the bodhi tree and entered nirvana along with the flowers of a pair of shala trees. He transmitted his Dharma to the honorable Mahakashyapa with a campala flower. Bodhidharma, our first Zen ancestor, opened five petals of one flower and celebrated the ever-lasting true Dharma, which has borne fruit ever since. Only This can pacify the evil and dangerous winds of 1970. In this way I have understood the meaning of the imperial poetic theme of this year, "flower."

> Buddha nature
> of a human, of a dog
> in full bloom

> Ima zo hito kushi busshō no hanazakari
> 今ぞ人狗子仏性の花さかり

JANUARY 1971

If you cannot return home, yourself is not your true self. Only when you fully arrive and return can you abide at ease. This year once again, spring and summer sesshin are scheduled at the Flower Sangha of California, the sanghas of New York, Hawaii, and London, the Pyramid Sangha of Cairo, and the Dead Sea Sangha of Jerusalem. Although the center of my heart is always in Japan, mine is a homeless home and a selfless self.

> Wherever I go
> is my home
> this Boar Year

> Itaru tokoro waga ya nari keri i shōgatsu
> いたるところわが家なりけり亥正月

JANUARY 1972

Zen practitioners at Myoshin-ji, Ryutaku-ji, Dai Bosatsu Zendo in New York, Kibutsu-ji in Jerusalem: Underneath your feet is the very peak of this earth. Aren't all people standing on top of

True Man without Rank

this great globe? May this understanding be a key point for the emancipation of humanity.

The Rat Year begins—
all children on this peak
are children of Buddha

Ne no haru no yama no ko minna hotoke no ko
子の春の山の子みんな佛の子

SPRING 1972

The path continues
endlessly
spring mountain

Haru no yama yuke ba michi ari doko made mo
春の山ゆけば道ありどこまでも

Finished, finished—when it is completely finished—there is nothing to finish

To Mui Shitsu [Eido Roshi] from Mitta Kutsu [Soen Roshi],
September 15, 1972, for official acknowledgment of *inka*

PART FOUR

INCREASING SECLUSION

1973–1984

Great bodhisattvas
small bodhisattvas
together begin the Ox Year

Daibosatsu kobosatsu tomoni ushi no haru
大ぼさつ小ぼさつともに丑の春

With Fuji in sight
I pick young herbs
that world and this world

Fuji mie te anoyo konoyo no wakana tsumu
不二見えてあの世この世の若菜つむ

[From "Ten Haiku of My Choice," 1973]
Fuji is represented by two characters that signify "wealthy person," but in the ancient Japanese text *Anthology of Ten Thousand Leaves* it was represented by the ideograms "not two." It has also been written as *fujin*, meaning inexhaustible; also as *fushi*, meaning no death. This world is no other than that world; that world is no other than this world.

Let me offer a haiku on the day of the ceremony for my successor to the abbotship. Today Sochu Suzuki becomes the eleventh abbot of Ryutaku-ji. As for me, I have been secluding myself more and more, like a bagworm.

Bagworm
has chosen his spot at last
inside the flower

Minomushi no tokoro sadame shi hana no naka
ミノ虫の所サダメシ花の中

June 3 is also the thirteenth anniversary of the death of our teacher, Gempo Roshi.

Two Poems for Gempo Yamamoto Roshi

Born deep in Kumano Province*
poling a raft and digging tree roots
he was almost blind
but through a mysterious unfolding
his true eye was opened.

Just now, just a person
just a free ride
just

Tadaima no tada ni tadanore tada no hito
只今の只に只乗れ只の人

JANUARY 1974

I am on a freighter from Yokohama, making my eleventh visit to the United States. Its capacity is twelve passengers, but there are only six of us on board. We have turned the empty cabins into a zendo, a tearoom, and a dance hall, and we have been having fun day and night. It's a sea-jacking! Namu dai bosa, Namu dai bosa!

A rainbow unfurls
over the Pacific Ocean—
tea ceremony!

Taiheiyō niji wo hirai te chanoyu kana
太平洋虹を開いて茶の湯かな

Winter sea
the arcing horizon
tips over

Fuyu no umi daienkyū wo katamukuru
冬の海大円球を傾くる

* *Kumano Province is the ancient name for a section of what is now known as Wakayama Prefecture.*

MARCH 28, 1974
Paramita Smile

Let True Dharma Continue, Universal Sangha Relations Become Complete! Due to the remarkable vow of young monk Eido, the New York Zendo was born in Manhattan in the fall of 1968; now, three years later, a gift has been made of fourteen hundred acres with a beautiful lake high in the remote Catskill Mountains of New York. The dream of an international DAIBOSATSU ZENDO [written thus in English] is at last about to come true. The lake is called Beecher Lake, and it was here that Harriet Beecher Stowe was inspired to write *Uncle Tom's Cabin*, which became an important factor in the emancipation of the slaves. My friend Father Nyokyu Maxima is now painting a large mural of Shakyamuni Buddha holding up a flower, with Mahakashyapa smiling. Indeed, from dawn to dusk, this is a spiritual mountain, a sacred lake. I will keep my ephemeral body here for a while, so that I may assist in the liberation of all beings.

> At night
> essence of flower
> becomes a firefly.
> In this remote mountain
> an American monastery.

MARCH 1974

> Snow of all countries
> melting into
> Namu dai bosa

> Kuniguni no yuki toke te namu dai bōsa
> 國々の雪溶けてなむだいぼーさ

JANUARY 1975

Tora ya ya! When the night of one billion worlds—of infinite dimensions—recedes, the realms of subtle and bright are indistinguishable. The mundane and the spiritual are not two. This three-dimensional, human realm is in the midst of another realm. Namu dai bosa! If we chant this mindfully, with admiration and joy, even once, our innumerable accumulated sins disappear. Shall we not dance? Shall we not sit with great rejoicing in the emerging of this paradise? Namu dai bosa, Namu dai bosa, Mu!

> Dance, humans and rabbits
> year's first festival
> bodhisattvas all!

> Hito mo u mo odore bosatsu no hatsumatsuri
> 人も卯もおどれ菩薩の初まつり

AUGUST 1975

On the morning of May 16, 1961, nineteen days before his passing away, I visited Gempo Roshi, who was convalescing at the hot springs of Takekura. He crawled out of bed and said, "Give me a brush." We students were flustered, and in consideration of his condition, we put one table on top of another and spread paper out for him. He said, "In that position, I don't have the strength to transmit my energy. Please take away the tables." He sat formally on the floor, as usual, and with the breath flowing through his entire body, he inscribed three large characters. He had been asked to write the characters for "birthplace," to be used on a stone to mark his native village at Unomine in Kumano. But instead, he wrote "Gempo's stupa," for his tombstone. Total birth, total death—Gempo Roshi vanished into vast space at age ninety-six. When I see his last calligraphy, I am overcome with tears, his image is so vividly before me. I remember his compassion—he only asked about my health, although he had been sick for three years.

> Summer birds
> shrieking in circles
> since that night

> Naki meguru natsu no tori ari sono yo yori
> 啼きめぐる夏の鳥ありその夜より

Namu Dai Bosa

To Know Death Prior to Death

JANUARY 1976

Ungan asked Tozan, "A monk asked Yakusan, 'I hear you are good at numbers. Is that true or not?' Yakusan said, 'Why don't you try this old monk?' The monk could not answer. What do you make of this?" Tozan said, "Please tell me the date you were born."

> Year of the Monkey:
> years of a life accumulating
> numberless

> Sarudoshi no nobi yuku ninju muryō kana
> 申年の伸びゆく人壽無量かな

JANUARY 1976

"Ascend to seek bodhi, descend to guide sentient beings": the path that goes up the mountain is the same path that goes down the mountain. When we want to guide sentient beings, we find that there are no sentient beings to guide. Step after step is nothing but Namu dai bosa, Namu dai bosa. At last on July 4 of this year, the bicentennial of the United States' independence, Kokusai-zan [International Mountain] Dai Bosatsu Zendo will officially open in the state of New York, in the nation of Earth.

> Emerging
> Bodhisattva mountain—
> in this bountiful light
> I shall dance
> the self of no-self.
> —Dragon Person, One Hundred Bows*

> Ascend the hill
> descend the hill
> dragon spring

> Nobore saka sono saka kudare ryū no haru
> 上れ坂その坂下れ龍の春

* After his retirement, Soen Nakagawa often used the name "Dragon Person" to sign his calligraphy and, sometimes, his poetry.

JANUARY 1977

It is said, "Fundamentally all sentient beings are becoming buddhas," but the expression "becoming buddhas" has a crack where
water leaks through. It is not that we are going to become a buddha in the future, but that we have been buddhas all along. At
the beginning of the Serpent Year, a new word, "Already-Buddha," came to me. In the entire universe, there is nothing but the
activities of Already-Buddha selfless-self. Namu dai bosa!

> Serpent self
> inexhaustible
> spring ocean

> Mi wa sudeni onore no umi zo haru mujin
> 巳は已に己の海ぞ春無盡

JANUARY 1978

This year's imperial theme is "mother." "Mother becomes more
and more a blessing, the older I grow," Gempo Yamamoto Roshi
often said. His eyes would grow moist just hearing the word
"mother." He was not only referring to his actual mother, of
course; a drop of water, a sheet of paper, the movement of a hand
or foot was the mother, the life of the universe.

JANUARY 1979

This old man was born in the Year of the Sheep and is now
celebrating the first day of the sixth cycle, but he is still very,
very immature. Every year I repeat solitary mountain retreats,
sometimes for a month, or for one hundred days. The year before
last I had a two hundred days' retreat, and last year I was the
master of one hundred and eight delusions and disappeared for
one hundred and eight days. This is still going on. I don't know
the self of this year. Namu dai bosa!

JANUARY 1980

On the emperor's poetic theme of the year, "cherry blossoms":

Cherry blossoms
neither open nor fall
eternal now

Sakura ima kairaku tomoni nakari keri
さくら今「開落」ともになかりけり

JUNE 1982

A great sesshin is held to mark the completion of the new zendo
at Entsu-zan [All-Pervading Mountain], Ryutaku-ji.

In the new zendo
all-pervading
fragrant breeze

Entsū ya shinzendō ni kaze kaoru
円通や新禪堂に風薫る

JANUARY 1983

The annual poetic theme is a koan given by the emperor to each
citizen in Yamato [the word for Japan, which also means great
harmony]. We should respond to this with our original voice,
through *waka,* haiku, or other works we are engaged in. We
should deepen our thoughts to transform the delusion not only
of the Japanese people, but of humanity as a whole, to bring
about the fruit of emancipation and the attainment of the Way.

On the emperor's poetic theme of the year, "Islands":

The Boar Year begins
a time for reshaping islands
Yamato!

I no haru ya ima zo Yamato no shimagatame
亥の春や今ぞ大和の島固め

JANUARY 1984

On the emperor's poetic theme of the year, "green":

Rat Year begins
emerald green shines
ever more brightly

Ne no haru zo mamidori iyoyo kagayaki te
子の春ぞ眞みどりいよよ輝きて

SPRING 1984

Death Poem

Mustard blossoms!
there is nothing left
to hurl away

Nanohana ya sarani nageutsu mono mo nashi
菜の花やさらに抛つものもなし

Let True Dharma Continue (Sho Bo Ku Ju)

POSTSCRIPT

"WHERE IS THE MASTER?"

by Roko Sherry Chayat

Soen Nakagawa Roshi's impact on Zen in the West was like a stone thrown in a shoreless lake: the ripples continue to expand. His formal teachings, through his teisho and dokusan, manifested his intimate rapport with the great Zen masters of old, particularly Rinzai and Bassui. His informal teachings, given while sitting in an airport, walking on a city street, or riding in a car, were playful yet no less serious. "*This* Matter, this life-and-death Matter," was to be realized with every breath.

During his visits to Zen groups in the United States, Israel, and other countries, he enthusiastically entered into students' ordinary lives. The spontaneous calligraphy he would offer his hosts, using scraps of paper and whatever writing implements were at hand; the impromptu tea ceremonies he would conduct with a styrofoam cup and instant coffee if that was all that was available—these were symbolic of the way he gave his Dharma away completely, over and over again.

His accessibility to Western practitioners, whether in their own countries or in Japan, was legendary. Ryutaku-ji was regarded as a mecca for foreign students during his abbotship; not only did Soen Roshi speak English, but he was sympathetic to these students' lack of familiarity with Japanese monastic etiquette and did everything he could—often at the expense of tradition—to make them feel welcome. Welcome, but not comfortable, for the power of his teaching was its element of surprise: every moment with him was an opportunity to wake up.

One of my earliest encounters with Soen Roshi was in the summer of 1971. I was attending my first week-long sesshin, which was held in those days in Litchfield, Connecticut, at a Catholic retreat center run by the Daughters of Wisdom. My first dokusan with Soen Roshi was about to occur, and I was absolutely terrified. Although I knew what to do upon entering the room—I had gone to dokusan with Tai-san, as Eido Roshi was then called, many times at the New York Zendo—I couldn't imagine actually speaking to this much-heralded Zen master who was visiting from Japan.

My turn came. Feeling entirely unworthy of Soen Roshi's time, I timidly struck the bell and walked up the stairs. I entered the dokusan room, but Soen Roshi's cushion was empty. Then I saw him, standing near the door, as though to pounce on me. "Come," he said. My mind raced. He had seen right through me! I wasn't going to be allowed to have dokusan!

He led me back down the stairs and stopped at the landing. As I was forlornly about to continue down, he said, "Wait! Come here." He was standing at the window. I went over to him, and he gently positioned me so that I was looking out. There was the enormous, deep-red ball of the sun bursting over the horizon! I had passed right by it on my way to see Roshi, thinking that dokusan had to take place in the dokusan room.

During the midseventies, I was a resident at International Dai Bosatsu Zendo. Soen Roshi arrived in August 1975, just after we had moved into the new monastery building, and spent several months there and at the New York Zendo. During Labor Day sesshin that year, in his first teisho in the new building, he presented the following poem:

> I came to open the door of Dai Bosatsu Zendo
> and found it was already open.
> I opened the book of Rinzai
> and found no word.
> Where is Master Rinzai?
> Where is the Master?
> Kwatz!

Soen Roshi changed people's lives. Many, many have written about the ways in which they were deeply touched by even a short encounter with him. Quite a few of these accounts were published in the *Soen Roku: The Sayings and Doings of Master Soen* (New York: The Zen Studies Society, 1986). Some of these practitioners have gone on to become Zen teachers and scholars; others have continued sitting, in little Zen groups and alone, in cities and quiet backwaters all around the world. Known and unknown, their steadfast determination can be attributed in no small part to Soen Roshi's continuing inspiration.

Ruth Strout McCandless met Soen Roshi in 1955, when she traveled with her teacher, Nyogen Senzaki, to Japan. She was the coauthor, with Senzaki, of *Buddhism and Zen* (San Francisco: North Point, 1953, 1987) and *The Iron Flute: One Hundred Zen Koan* (Rutland, Vt.: Charles Tuttle Co., 1964, 1985). On that first trip to Japan, she attended sesshin at Ryutaku-ji and spent six weeks with Soen Roshi, a period she has described as "far beyond anything as ephemeral as happiness." The following is from her account of her visits with him in Japan and, later, in the United States:

Wherever we were, Soen Roshi was always teaching and testing. He seldom instructed, and never lectured. Sometimes there was not even a phrase or a word, but there was never any doubt as to what was meant.

People responded to him instantly—on the train, in the park, everywhere he went—but there was never any egocentrically used charm. He loved people, animals, nature. Senzaki Sensei once said to me that Soen Roshi was pure love. He was, indeed. And, of course, animals as well as people were aware of it. I remember going with him to visit a student in California. The household owned a vicious dog, trained to attack. When we arrived, I saw that the dog was in their fenced garden, but they had forgotten to lock him up. Before I could warn Soen Roshi, he was out of the car and had entered the garden. And the dog? He was bouncing happily around Soen Roshi, wagging his tail and licking Roshi's hand. . . .

Soyen Shaku Roshi . . . Daisetz Suzuki . . . Nyogen Senzaki . . . Soen Roshi . . . Eido Roshi. The eastbound teaching moves on.

Where the light is brightest
The shadows are sharpest.*

* A translation by Ruth McCandless of a poem by Soen Roshi.

The renowned writer and Zen teacher Peter Matthiessen offered this from his journal of August 1975:

Cleaning the zendo after evening sitting, I find Soen alone in the shadows at the end of the empty row, in the stillness of zazen. He is the archetypal old monk of the paintings, ancient as death, burning with life. I dust around him. These days his joy in life is dark; he refers gleefully to "the majority," as he calls the dead. . . . Each day he reminds us that, despite all the tumult and delusion of our life, our true nature is always there, like the sun or moon above black wind and clouds. "The sun is shining; the sun is *always* shining. The sun is enlightenment; everything is enlightenment!" He dabbles his fingers in a water bowl. "Do you hear? *That is enlightenment!*" At one point he reads his own new haiku:

In the midst of winter
I find in myself at last
Invincible summer.

Brenda Lukeman, a writer, therapist, and long-time practitioner at the New York Zendo Shobo-ji, remembers Soen Roshi thus:

At Soen's side, I felt that great enlightenment was possible, that it was only around the corner. I felt that it was simple, and that it also could be fun.

Soen would disappear a lot. We would all be expecting him and he wouldn't come. If you wanted to hold on to him, you were in trouble! What could we hold on to then?

"Hold on to Mu," Soen whispered to me in my ear one day. "Is that all?" I asked him, and he grinned.

He taught without teaching, and I learned without knowing I was learning anything. Just being together, moment by moment, just one breath after another. There was nothing much more to do. It was so simple, it was impossible to grasp.

"Whatever you do is a waste of time," he said to me one day, "until you have great enlightenment. Even reading the newspaper is a waste of time. Once you have great enlightenment, every newspaper becomes a sutra. When your mind is clear enough, even a squirrel becomes your wonderful teacher."

Mick Sopko, now chief baker at San Francisco Zen Center's Green Gulch Farm in California, was a resident at the New York Zendo Shobo-ji during the 1970s. He recalls:

Soen Roshi's voice was unlike anything I had ever heard, or indeed have heard since. It was hard to believe such a deep and penetrating sound could come from such a frail-looking instrument. His voice embodied the many subtleties of tenderness, aspiration, and wonder.

For some reason, I've clearly preserved a memory of him in the kitchen at the New York Zendo. It was twilight. He was working at the counter, cracking open gingko nuts and taking out the kernels in order to roast them. He'd enlisted the aid of many of us to gather the foul-smelling nuts from all over the city and bring them to the zendo, where he worked on them—hundreds of them. When roasted, they would turn emerald green and were very tasty. He'd keep them in the sleeves of his robes to give to visitors.

The sight of him there in the half-light touched me deeply. All alone, in his tattered golden robes, in the midst of that powerful stench, he toiled over the tiny kernels that would become gifts.

Soen Roshi seemed to come from an ancient world. He flew in planes, took trains, cars, and boats all over the place, but he seemed mainly to be walking. He didn't care much for electric lights, and encouraged us to be particularly observant at dawn and dusk. He roamed through the predawn city streets, gazing up at the illuminated, iconic skyscrapers, looking in dumpsters, gathering bits of vegetation from along the sidewalks that bordered the East River to sprinkle over his breakfast gruel. When we were at Dai Bosatsu Zendo, we could sometimes hear him early in the morning before zazen, splashing in the dark, cold lake, and singing in his solemn Noh manner: bringing up the sun.

One afternoon he called Ray, my fellow resident, and me into his room. Large sheets of rice paper were spread out on newspapers all over the tatami. He had his sleeves rolled back and was chanting

"Namu dai bosa"; he looked like a character from a Kurosawa movie. Ray and I and two rocks held down the corners of a scroll-size sheet of paper; Soen stood above us, chanting and dipping his large brush into the ink. He suddenly lunged forward, pulling a thick diagonal line up the paper—and then kept on going, tumbling over onto the tatami. He jumped right up again and made a horizontal squiggle, and another diagonal going down. "Mount Fuji," he said. It was clear that this wasn't merely a representation; it was the mountain itself.

Soen Roshi harbored a dark and mysterious energy. During one sesshin at Dai Bosatsu Zendo, after dokusan, he was sitting facing the wall when a raccoon entered through an open door. Soen Roshi turned to look at it, across a distance of about twenty-five feet. Their gazes locked for about a minute. The raccoon became more and more skittish; then, its sharp teeth chattering, it spun around and ran off. Another time, he retreated to his room at the New York Zendo and went unseen for several weeks. We would leave trays of food outside his door. When he emerged, his hair and fingernails had grown long. He said he had "been to hell," and he cautioned us to stay out of the room for a few days because there were still demons in there.

It's been more than twenty years since I've seen Soen Roshi, yet hardly a day goes by that I don't recall some incident involving him. Why is this? He never really had much to say to me, and I can't say I "understood" many of his talks. I was shy and nervous in his presence, and I doubt if I asked him many questions of an existential nature. But in the years since, when such questions have become more important to me, I've often asked myself, "What would Soen say or do in this situation?" This means, "What is the natural thing to do?" or "What do I really feel?"

Soen Roshi seemed to be acting from a place that was free from ambivalence, so that the smallest thing he did or said had the power to carry backward and forward in time.

Louis Nordstrom, a Zen teacher, scholar, and poet, was head monk at Dai Bosatsu Zendo during the midseventies. He writes:

> I loved Soen Roshi, but who was he? What manner of being? To be in his overwhelming presence was in all earnestness to ask this

sort of question—and always to have no idea! Had he in his pilgrimaging traveled, so to speak, beyond the human (whatever that might mean)? One somehow got this impression; but at the same time, one felt that he was Nietzsche's *ecce homo*—human, all-too-human. Only from a rational point of view are these two separate, however. Are going beyond the human and being completely human not-two? Soen Roshi embodied this paradox. Might he have said, "Indeed, I am not a human being"? He was a formidable koan indeed. Looking into his eyes I always felt as if I were peering into a cave (and Mitta Kutsu, Cave of the Paramitas, was the name Gempo Roshi had bestowed upon him). It was as if there were no one at home. Or as Soen Roshi expressed it, "No one at home—yet no vacancy!" (The occasion for this was his seeing a No Vacancy sign in front of a motel.)

And yet, and yet . . . the incomparable joy he inspired. His fabulously innocent smile. The great laughter. The sheer hilarity drinking sake with him after crazy "Namu dai bosa" dancing and "Kanzeon" chanting at Shobo-ji the last time I saw him, during his last visit to America in 1982. Laughing Shiva.

I have seen his face express an almost frightening depth of melancholy, a cosmic sadness, if you will. His impenetrably dark, masklike face always reminded me of Nietzsche's remark that when you stare into the abyss, the abyss stares back at you. Masks—Soen loved them. I remember once I was shaving his head. We were looking into the mirror and our eyes met, and he said, "I'll take off my mask if you take off yours!"

How well I remember the bottomless mirth with which he invariably greeted neurotic presentations of self! In his presence, indeed, it seemed crazy to think in terms of "problems" at all. Soen Roshi embodied at all times the penetrating wisdom of "Everything is OK!" What is this "OK"? It is his precious legacy. It is easy for American Zen students to prattle about the Way being all-inclusive, even beyond good and evil, but ironically, when we encounter as close an approximation to an incarnation of this all-inclusive Way as Soen Roshi, we are dumbfounded that there could be such wild, crazy teaching. Of all the Zen teachers I have known and studied with, Soen Roshi without question came closest to embodying the

Way in this all-inclusive, nothing-excluded sense. "Any way OK!" he would say. Or again:

All is revealed as it is now.
All is realized as it is now.
All is enlightened as it is now.
OK!

Soen Roshi's final years were difficult ones. Along with the chronic pain resulting from his accident, he often seemed in the grip of an overwhelming sadness. Although he could be exuberant and took a childlike delight in the unexpected and unconventional, he was uncompromising in his moral standards. He was severe and unyielding with regard to anything he felt was polluting the Dharma and was particularly hard on himself. For example, after reading a transcription of his own teisho, he shook his head sadly and said, "Lies, lies." He had little patience with human frailties in the realm of relationships. After his retirement from the abbotship of Ryutaku-ji, he felt increasingly isolated. Suffering from more frequent bouts of depression, he turned to the path he had so often chosen as a young monk: okomori, solitary retreat.

In one of his last teisho at Dai Bosatsu Zendo, he spoke of the precious gift of being born as a human. To honor this gift, he said, we must continually vow to extinguish our inexhaustible delusions; we must continually realize that the sun is shining on a day black with clouds. This is our endless vow.

October 2, 1995
Zen Center of Syracuse Hoen-ji
Syracuse, New York

CHRONOLOGY

1907 Born March 19 in Keelung, Formosa (now Taiwan), to an army physician, Dr. Suketaro Nakagawa, and his wife, Kazuko, and given the name Motoi.
Family moves to Iwakune and then to Hiroshima.

1917 Father dies.

1923 Enters First Academy in Tokyo.

1927 Enters Tokyo Imperial University; lives in dormitory at Gangyo-ji, a Pure Land temple.

1931 Completes graduate school at Tokyo Imperial University.
Ordained March 19 by Keigaku Katsube Roshi at Kogaku-ji.
Begins solitary retreats on Mount Dai Bosatsu.
Becomes a student of haiku master Dakotsu Iida.

1932 Conceives of International Dai Bosatsu Zendo and travels to Sakhalin Island to search for gold in order to fund the project.
Shubin Tanahashi becomes a student of Nyogen Senzaki.
Eido Tai Shimano is born in Nakano, Arai, a district of Tokyo.

1933 Completes *Shigan* (Coffin of Poems).

1934 Poems and essays from *Shigan* (Coffin of Poems) printed in *Fujin Koron*.

1935 Hears Gempo Yamamoto Roshi's teisho at Hakusan Dojo; later has private meeting with him and is invited to be his student at Ryutaku-ji and in Manchuria.
Correspondence with Nyogen Senzaki begins.

1937   First trip to Manchuria with Gempo Roshi.

1939   Solitary retreat on Mount Dai Bosatsu.

1941   Ryutaku-ji is officially acknowledged as a monastic training center. War in the Pacific starts.

1945   War in the Pacific ends.

1949   First of thirteen trips to the United States. Publishes *Meihen* (Life Anthology).

1951   Installed as abbot of Ryutaku-ji.

1954   Meets a young monk, Tai Shimano, at funeral service for Dai-kyu Mineo Roshi; that summer, the monk becomes his student at Ryutaku-ji.

1955   Second visit to the United States.
        That September, Nyogen Senzaki returns to Japan for the first time since his departure in 1905; visits Ryutaku-ji during his six-week stay.

1957   Death of Soen Roshi's ordination teacher, Keigaku Katsube Roshi.

1958   Death of Nyogen Senzaki; third trip to the United States, to settle Senzaki's affairs, having been named the executor of his estate.

1959   Fourth trip to the United States.

1960   Fifth trip to the United States; flies to Honolulu, Hawaii, to lead first sesshin there.
        Eido Tai Shimano's arrival in the United States.

1961   Death of Gempo Yamamoto Roshi.

1962   Mother dies.

1963   Travels around the world with Charles Gooding, one of Nyogen Senzaki's students. Visits the United States, India, Israel, Egypt, England, Austria, and Denmark, flying over the Arctic Circle on his way back to Japan.
        Underground plumbing system installed at Ryutaku-ji.

1966   Engages in fundraising to acquire land surrounding Ryutaku-ji.

1967   Near-fatal accident.

1968   Seventh visit to the United States; with him in the ship's hold is the Amitabha Buddha image from main altar at Ryutaku-ji, to be installed on the main altar of New York Zendo Shobo-ji, which opens September 15.

1969   Travels to sesshin at sanghas in Israel, England, Egypt, and the United States (New York, California, and Hawaii).

1971   Ninth visit to the United States.
Zen Studies Society purchases fourteen hundred acres in the Catskill Mountains for International Dai Bosatsu Zendo.

1972   Tenth visit to the United States.

1973   Retires from abbotship of Ryutaku-ji.
Publication of "Ten Haiku of My Choice."

1974   Eleventh visit to the United States, to stay at International Dai Bosatsu Zendo with Father Nyokyu Maxima, who paints a mural there.

1975   Twelfth visit to the United States; gives first teisho in new monastery building; that fall, goes into solitary retreat at New York Zendo Shobo-ji.

1976   Official opening of International Dai Bosatsu Zendo.
One-hundredth anniversary of Nyogen Senzaki's birth.

1981   Publishes *Henkairoku* (Journal of a Wide World) with *Kounsho* (Ancient Cloud Selection).

1982   Last visit to the United States.

1984   March 11, departure.

GLOSSARY

In the following entries, S. = Sanskrit, J. = Japanese, and C. = Chinese.

AMITĀBHA (S.; J. Amida) The Buddha of Infinite Light, who presides in what is variously called the Western Paradise, Sukhā-vati, or the Pure Land. Amida is venerated in Pure Land Buddhism through the repetition of the mantra "Namu Amida Butsu," meaning "homage to Amida Buddha." See Jōdo Shū.

AVALOKITESHVARA (S. Avalokiteśvara; J. Kannon or Kanzeon) The bodhisattva who sees the suffering of all beings, who hears all cries. Avalokiteshvara is the embodiment of compassion, just as Manjushri is the embodiment of wisdom. Iconographically, Avalokiteshvara is often depicted with a thousand arms, with an eye in the palm of each hand, and with eleven faces. See bodhisattva.

AVATAMSAKA-SŪTRA (S.) The Flower Garland Sutra, a Mahāyāna scripture that contains the teachings upon which the Chinese Hua-yen School is based. It emphasizes mutually unobstructed interpenetration and the identity of the human mind, Buddha, and all sentient beings.

BASHŌ Matsuo Bashō (1644–1694) was one of the greatest haiku poets in Japanese history. He established the haiku form and was known especially for his journals and poems based on his travels. He was a Zen practitioner.

BASSUI   Bassui Tokushō was born in Sagami Province, Japan, in 1327. He went to study under Zen Master Ōkō at Jifuku-ji when he was about twenty years old. He shaved his head at the age of twenty-nine, but rejected the religious establishment of his day, neither wearing robes nor reciting sutras. His dedication to zazen was uncompromising. His realization occurred when, after sitting through the night, he heard the sound of the mountain stream at dawn. Later, with Kohō Kakumyō, he had an even more profound awakening, and he studied with many other renowned masters. He never remained with any of them, living instead in a series of hermitages. Eventually the number of students surrounding him became so great that Kōgaku-an was established, where more than one thousand monks and laypersons were under his tutelage. His key teaching was "What is This? Who is hearing this sound?" and his final words, spoken in 1387, were: "Look directly! What is This? Look in this manner and you won't be fooled."

BEECHER LAKE   The highest lake in the Catskill Mountains of New York State, on the banks of which is located International Dai Bosatsu Zendo. The influential nineteenth-century spiritual leader Henry Ward Beecher had a house there for private retreats; his sister, Harriet Beecher Stowe, may have written part of *Uncle Tom's Cabin* there.

BHIKSHU, BHIKSHUNI   (S. *bhikṣu, bhikṣunī*)   Monks and nuns.

BODHI (S.)   Perfect wisdom; enlightenment; awakening to one's own Buddha nature.

BODHICITTA   (S.)   Literally, awakened mind.

BODHIDHARMA   (S.; J. Bodaidaruma or Daruma)   The twenty-eighth master after Shakyamuni in the Indian lineage, who traveled from India to China in 520 CE and is considered the first ancestral teacher of Zen. He emphasized the direct experience of seeing into one's true nature rather than relying on scriptures or the formulations of others.

BODHISATTVA   (S.; J. *bosatsu* or *bosa*)   An enlightened being who understands realization not as a personal goal, not as an end in itself, but as a means to liberate all beings from suffering, and who dedicates her- or himself to manifesting compassion and wisdom in daily life.

BUDDHA   (S.)   Literally, enlightened one. The historical Buddha is Shakyamuni Buddha (563–483 BCE). The son of a prince of the Shakya clan, his personal name was Siddhārtha Gautama. Through his awakening he realized that fundamentally all beings are buddhas; and that there is a path of liberation that can be taught, received, and followed. The term is also used to refer to buddhas who preceded Shakyamuni, like his teacher, Dīpaṅkara; and to the buddha who will renew the Dharma in the future age, Maitreya. There are also buddhas, like Amitābha and Vairocana, who are held to be teachers of the bodhisattvas; each is the mystical personification of a Pure Land.

BUDDHA DHARMA   (S.)   Buddha teaching, or fundamental law, which cannot be understood conceptually but must be grasped intuitively through the experience of enlightenment. The manifestation of true nature in all phenomena. See Dharma.

CARLSON, CHESTER   The primary benefactor of the Zen Studies Society. Inventor of the Xerox photocopying process, he and his wife, Dorris, made it possible for the society to purchase the New York City carriage house that became the New York Zendō Shōbō-ji and to establish its country retreat center, International Dai Bosatsu Zendō.

DAI BOSATSU   (J.)   Literally, Great or All-Encompassing Bodhisattva. See Namu dai bosa.

DAI BOSATSU, MOUNT   The mountain in Yamanashi Prefecture where Sōen Nakagawa spent much of his time as a young monk; known for its fine view of Mount Fuji.

DAI BOSATSU PASS   The pass on Mount Dai Bosatsu in Yamanashi Prefecture, Japan, surrounded by the peaks of Fuji, Yari, Hodaka, Jizo, Shaka, and Shirane.

DAITŌ KOKUSHI   The posthumous honorific title given to the Japanese Zen master Shūhō Myōchō (1282–1338), founder of Daitoku-ji and the teacher of Kanzan Egen. He was made the Dharma successor to Jyōmyō and then lived for a time among the beggars under Kyōto's Gojō Bridge before settling in a hermitage on a hill in the outskirts of Kyōto. Eventually, because of the great number of students who gathered around him, Daitoko-ji was established there. *Kokushi* means "national teacher."

166   GLOSSARY

DAITOKU-JI   A monastery in Kyōto founded by Daitō Kokushi; one of the headquarters of the Rinzai School.

DHARMA   (S.)   A key term in Buddhism with many meanings, the first of which is "thing" or "phenomenon." Physical phenomena and mental constructs are subject to the law of causation; another meaning of Dharma is law, or truth. Still another meaning is the teachings of the Buddha, whose realization penetrated into the fundamental truth of the universe.

DHARMAKĀYA BUDDHA   The condition of buddhahood that is identical with ultimate reality; the emanation as formlessness.

DIAMOND SŪTRA   (S., *Vajracchedikā-prajñāpāramitā-sūtra*)   Literally, Sutra of the Diamond-Cutter of Supreme Wisdom, it is a key section of the *Prajñāpāramitā-sūtra* literature, teaching that all phenomenal appearances are illusory projections of the mind, with no fixed identity.

DŌGEN   Eihei Dōgen (1200–1253) trained for nine years under the Rinzai master Myōan Eisai before traveling to China, where he studied with and became the Dharma heir of Tendō Nyojō (C. T'ien-t'ung Ju-ching). He brought the teachings of the Sōtō (C. Ts'ao-tung) school of Zen from China back to Japan and he established Eihei-ji, which became the principal Sōtō training monastery. Dōgen wrote many important essays on Zen, the best-known collection of which is the *Shōbōgenzō* (Treasury of the True Dharma Eye). In this teaching he criticized what he saw as signs of degeneration and formulaic practices among Rinzai adherents; he stressed the importance of zazen as the sole route to enlightenment—and at the same time, warned against striving for enlightenment. *See* Sōtō.

DOKUSAN   (J.)   Private, formal encounters between teacher and student, particularly important in Rinzai Zen practice; usually held two or three times a day during sesshin.

DŌRIN   (C. Tao-lin)   Known as Bird's Nest Rōshi because he often did zazen in a tree.

FUJIMORI, KŌZEN   Trained at Ryūtaku-ji and became one of Sōen Nakagawa's successors. He went on to become abbot of Hōkō-ji, one of the headquarters of the Rinzai School.

GASSHŌ   (J.)   The gesture of reverence, of greeting, of gratitude, and of expressing oneness with all beings, made by putting the palms of the hands together.

GANGYŌ-JI   The Jōdo Shū (Pure Land) temple in Tōkyō where Sōen Nakagawa lived for three years while studying at Tōkyō Imperial University.

GATELESS GATE   (J. *Mumonkan;* C. *Wu-men-kuan*)   One of the key kōan collections, compiled by Mumon Ekai (C. Wu-men Hui-k'ai) and published in 1229. *See* Mumon Ekai.

GYŌKI   (d. 749 CE)   Considered an incarnation of Manjushri Bodhisattva, he traveled all over Japan. At Mount Dai Bosatsu he set up a shrine to a deity called a Daigongen, or Great Avatar, a manifestation of Dharmakāya Buddha.

HAIKU   A Japanese poetic form written in seventeen syllables consisting of units of five, seven, and five. It is usually written in one vertical line of calligraphy, but sometimes, for visual effect, in two or more lines. A basic requirement is a word or phrase that indicates the season.

HAKUIN   Hakuin Ekaku (1685–1768) was the Zen master who revived Rinzai Zen in Japan, remodeled the Rinzai kōan system, and was the honorary founder of Ryūtaku-ji. His genius manifested itself in teaching, writing, and painting.

HARA   (J.)   Also known as *kikai tanden,* it refers both to the physical center of the body and to the locus of spiritual power in the lower abdomen. Regulating the breath so that it is focused in the hara results in the accumulation of samādhi energy essential to zazen and fosters the experiential understanding that mind and body are one.

HARADA, SŌGAKU   An outstanding Zen teacher (1870–1961) whose instructions for beginners in Zen became known through his student and Dharma successor Hakuun Yasutani, whose lectures based on those instructions were translated into English by Philip Kapleau in *Three Pillars of Zen.*

HEART SŪTRA   (S., *Mahāprajñāpāramitā-hridaya-sūtra*)   The Heart of Perfect Wisdom Sūtra, one of the most important sūtras of Mahāyāna Buddhism. It is recited daily by practitioners of many schools of Buddhism and is particularly emphasized in Zen for its clear and concise teaching of *shunyata* (emptiness).

HEIRIN-JI   The temple near Tōkyō where Eidō Shimano first began his training, under Keizan Shirouzu.

HOSSHIN-JI   A temple in Obama, Fukui Prefecture, known for its rigorous training; its abbot was Sōgaku Harada.

IIDA, DAKOTSU   A well-known haiku master (1885–1962) with whom Sōen Nakagawa studied.

INJI   (J.) A teacher's attendant.

ISSA   Issa Kobayashi (1766–1827), a haiku poet.

JIKIJITSU   (J.) The leader and timekeeper of the zendō in Rinzai Zen, responsible for maintaining a strong and alert atmosphere. Literally, *jiki* means "straight," and *jitsu* means "day," implying one who sits straight through the entire day.

JIZŌ   (J.; S. Ksitigarbha)   A bodhisattva venerated as the protector of children, travelers, and vulnerable people in general. He is the only bodhisattva portrayed as a monk, often with a staff and a *mani* (wish-fulfilling) jewel.

JŌDO SHŪ   (J.)   School of the Pure Land. Its followers place absolute trust in Amida Buddha (S. Amitābha), as do adherents of the Jōdo Shin Shū (True School of the Pure Land). The teaching emphasizes that the sincere and repetitive recitation of the formula "Namu Amida Butsu" will result in rebirth as a buddha in the Pure Land. For the Jōdo Shū adherent, the recitation itself deepens the trust in Amida. *See* Amitābha.

JOHNSTONE, WILLIAM   A brilliant businessman who spent much of his life administering Bethlehem Steel and who was chair of the building committee of International Dai Bosatsu Zendō.

JŌSHŪ JŪSHIN   (J.; C. Chao-chou Ts'ung-shen)   Jōshū (778–897) experienced profound enlightenment at the age of eighteen. He then trained for forty more years under Nansen Fugan (C. Nan-ch'uan P'u-yuan), and after Nansen's death he made pilgrimages to deepen his realization further. He did not begin teaching until the age of eighty, when he settled in a small monastery in the province of Chao-chou. He is best known through the kōan in which he answered a monk's question, "Does a dog have Buddha nature or not?" with the succinct reply, "Mu!" (Case 1 of the *Gateless Gate*). *See* Mu.

JUKAI   (J.)   The ceremony in which a lay practitioner receives the precepts of Buddhism, ethical guidelines governing behavior, and dedicates her- or himself to the path.

KAJIURA, ITSUGAI   Itsugai Kajiura (1896–1981) was abbot of Myōshin-ji and before that, of Shōgen-ji.

KANNON   See Avalokiteshvara.

KANZAN EGEN   Also known as Musō Daishi (1277–1360). After he received Dharma transmission from Shūhō Myōchō (Daitō Kokushi), he spent many years in the mountains in order to deepen his realization. He worked as a laborer by day and did zazen at night. He founded Myōshin-ji and Shōgen-ji.

KANZEON   See Avalokiteshvara.

KATSUBE, KEIGAKU   From the 1920s until his death in 1957, Keigaku Katsube was abbot of Kōgaku-ji, the monastery founded by Bassui. Sōen (Motoi) Nakagawa, while a graduate student at Tōkyō University, attended one of Keigaku Rōshi's public zazen meetings at Shōrin-ji; in 1931 Keigaku Rōshi ordained Motoi and gave him the Buddhist name Sōen. See Kōgaku-ji.

KEISAKU   (J., also kyōsaku)   A long, flat, wooden stick used during zazen periods to rouse sleepy practitioners, to provide relief from muscle tension and fatigue, and to intensify the atmosphere.

KENSHŌ   (J., also satori)   An essential element in Rinzai Zen, usually translated as realization, awakening, or enlightenment. Kenshō refers to the liberating experience of breaking through the ego-driven, self-preoccupied view of reality to the clear understanding of things just as they are. Ken means "seeing into," shō means "one's own nature."

KESA   (J.; transliteration of S. kaṣāya)   A ceremonial robe used by fully ordained practitioners. Draped over the left shoulder, the kesa is symbolic of the patchwork garment worn by monks in India during Shakyamuni Buddha's time. The abbreviated version used during zazen and other nonceremonial activities is the rakusu, worn over the chest. See rakusu.

KESSEI   (J.)   Three-month training period in a Zen monastery, also called ango.

KINHIN   (J.)   Walking meditation done between periods of zazen, symbolic of the transition between motionless practice and the practice of daily life.

170   GLOSSARY

KŌAN (J.) Literally, public case, taken from the Chinese *kung-an*. A key element of Rinzai Zen practice and sometimes used in the Sōtō School as well, a kōan is constructed from a recorded encounter between a master and a student, a sūtra, or a teaching, and is used to spur the practitioner toward breaking free of habitual responses and intellectual concepts. Kōans cannot be solved by logical analysis; they require full-bore intuitive concentration. Intensive kōan practice, particularly during sesshin, can result in self-realization. *See* kenshō.

KŌGAKU-JI The temple in Enzan, Yamanashi Prefecture, founded by Bassui, where Sōen Nakagawa was ordained by Keigaku Katsube in 1931.

KOTO A Japanese harp placed flat on the floor when played.

KWATZ! Rinzai's famous shout, used by Zen masters in the Rinzai School to cut through delusions. *See* Rinzai.

KYŌGEN CHIKAN (J.; C. Hsiang-yen Chih-hsien) An accomplished scholar who studied with Hyakujō Ekai (C. Pai-chang Huai-hai). After his teacher's death he became a student of Isan Reiyū (C. Kuei-shan Ling-yu). When the latter asked him about his "original face before his parents were born," he found that all his scholarly writings were of no avail, burned his books, and withdrew to a hermitage at Nanyō (C. Nan-yang). While sweeping one day, his broom hit a pebble; the sound it made hitting a bamboo tree triggered Kyōgen's realization.

MAHAKASHYAPA (S. Mahākāśyapa) Shakyamuni Buddha's senior disciple and successor, who received wordless transmission when, upon seeing the Buddha holding aloft a flower, he smiled.

MAHĀYĀNA (S.) Literally, Great Vehicle, referring to its emphasis on attaining liberation for the sake of all beings, thus broadening the scope of early Buddhism, with its emphasis on individual realization. Zen is one of the schools based in the Mahāyāna branch of Buddhism. The Mahāyāna view is that one's true nature is from the beginning liberated; the realization and actualization of this are embodied in the way of the bodhisattva.

MAṆḌALA (S.) Literally, circle or section, a maṇḍala is a symbolic representation of the spiritual world, conveying the subtle interweaving of form and nonform, being and nonbeing.

MANJUSHRI   (S. Mañjuśrī; J. Monju)   Literally, the noble and gentle one. The bodhisattva of wisdom, he is often depicted with an ignorance-dispelling sword in his right hand and a volume of the *Prajñāpāramitā* literature in his left.

MANTRA   A mystical verse, like "Namu dai bosa."

MAXIMA, NYOKYŪ   A priest of the Russian Orthodox Church who painted murals combining Western and Eastern aesthetic principles. One such mural was created at International Dai Bosatsu Zendō when he visited the United States with Sōen Nakagawa.

McCANDLESS, RUTH STROUT (1909–1994)   Became a student of Nyogen Senzaki in 1940. In 1941 he gave her the Dharma name Kangetsu. She collaborated with Senzaki on *Buddhism and Zen* and *The Iron Flute: One Hundred Zen Koan.* When Senzaki was interned in a camp during World War II, he entrusted her with all his books and important possessions. She traveled with him to Japan in 1955 and spent six weeks with Sōen Nakagawa, and returned in later years.

MEIBAKU HUT   The rustic structure in which Sōen Nakagawa lived while doing solitary retreats on Mount Dai Bosatsu.

MU   (J.; Ch. *wu*)   The syllable Zen students know best, from case 1 of the *Gateless Gate:* A monk asked Jōshū (C. Chao-chou), "Does a dog have Buddha nature or not?" Jōshū answered, "Mu!" Literally, *mu* means no, none, or nothing; logically, of course, such an answer goes against what the monk has been taught: that all beings have Buddha nature. In Zen practice, Mu is used to delve deeply into the profundity of this "no."

MUMON EKAI   (J.; C. Wu-men Hui-k'ai)   Mumon (1183–1260) compiled the *Gateless Gate* (J. *Mumonkan;* C. *Wu-men-kuan*), a collection of forty-eight kōans for which he wrote the accompanying commentaries and verses. His own six-year struggle with Mu resulted in a profound awakening, and later, when he composed the *Gateless Gate,* he made "Jōshū's 'Mu'" the first case in that collection. His disciple and Dharma successor Shinchi Kakushin brought a copy of the *Gateless Gate,* written in Mumon's own hand, back to Japan with him in 1254.

MUMONKAN   *See* Gateless Gate.

MYŌSHIN-JI   A monastery in Kyōto founded by Kanzan Egen that serves as one of the headquarters of the Rinzai School.

NAMU DAI BOSA   A mantra (mystical verse) chanted almost continually by Sōen Nakagawa, it can be translated as "Homage to the great Bodhisattva." Its meaning is to become one with the boundless Bodhisattva spirit that is our intrinsic nature. "Dai bosa" is the shortened, chanted form of Dai Bosatsu.

NANSEN FUGAN   (J.; C. Nan-ch'uan P'u-yuan)   Dharma heir of Baso Dōitsu (C. Ma-tsu Tao-i), Nansen (748–835) was one of the most important Zen masters of the T'ang dynasty, renowned for his dynamic and paradoxical way of expressing his understanding. Among his seventeen Dharma successors was Jōshū Jūshin (C. Chao-chou Ts'ung-shen).

NEN   (J.)   Literally, "present heart-mind." Intensive mind; consciousness vibrantly at one with the present moment.

NICHIREN   Founder of the Nichiren School of Buddhism in Japan, which is based on the teachings of the *Lotus Sutra*. Nichiren (1222–1282) said those teachings alone could save humankind during a period of religious decline, and that the recitation of the sutra's title alone, "Namu myō hō ren ge kyō" ("Veneration to the Sutra of the Lotus of the Inconceivable Law"), could lead to liberation. He was exiled to the island of Sado for his criticism of other Buddhist schools; in 1274, he was allowed to return to Kamakura.

NOH   A highly stylized form of Japanese medieval drama; in the past, often practiced and patronized by the warrior class. Actors, often masked and in elaborate costumes, perform accompanied by a chorus and musicians.

NIRVĀṆA   (S.)   Literally, extinction. In Mahāyāna Buddhism, often regarded as extinction of the dualistic views (including birth and death) that cause suffering. A condition beyond conceptualization in which the identity of the relative and the absolute is experienced. *See* Parinirvāṇa.

PĀRAMITĀ   (S.)   Literally, having reached the Other Shore, a metaphor for crossing the ocean of suffering to arrive at the shore of enlightenment. The six pāramitās are the perfections, or virtues, characteristic of a bodhisattva: *dāna* (generosity); *śīla* (morality or precepts), *kṣānti* (patience or tolerance), *vīrya* (diligence), *dhyāna* (meditation), and *prajñā* (wisdom). By practicing the pāramitās, the Other Shore is realized to be none other than this shore, the here and now.

PARINIRVĀṆA   (S.)   Total extinction: usually refers to Shakyamuni Buddha's passing away.

PRAJÑĀ   (S.)   Wisdom or intuitive mind. Prajñā is the sixth pāramitā. In Zen, it is not held to be some separate condition to be attained as a result of dhyāna (meditation), but rather it is the simultaneous functioning of dhyāna.

RAKUSU   (J.)   A rectangular, pieced-together vestment worn by monks, nuns, and lay Buddhists. The rakusu hangs on the chest from a strap around the neck. Symbolic of the patched robes worn by Shakyamuni Buddha and his disciples, and received when taking the precepts, the rakusu is the abbreviated form of the kesa (which is worn only by monks and nuns). *See* kesa.

REKIJŪ KAIDŌ   (J.)   A one-day ceremony in which a highly regarded Zen master is made honorary abbot of one of the Rinzai headquarters.

REPS, PAUL   An American Zen practitioner, author, and poet (1895–1990) who collaborated with Nyogen Senzaki on *Zen Flesh, Zen Bones.*

RIKYŪ   Sen-no-Rikyū, or Rikyū of the Sen family (1520–1591), established the tea ceremony in Japan.

RINZAI   (J.; C. Lin-chi)   Chinshu Rinzai Gigen, who died in 866 or 867, founded what became the most influential Buddhist sect of T'ang-dynasty China, the Lin-chi School. Rinzai and Sōtō Zen are the two major schools of Zen in Japan and the West. Rinzai was known for his abrupt and dynamic methods of awakening students, which included shouts ("Kwatz!") and unexpected blows. His training style was the culmination of Zen's development from Enō (J.; C. Hui-neng) through Ōbaku (J.; C. Huang-po), from whom he received Dharma transmission. Rinzai had twenty-one successors, and appears in cases 20 and 32 of the *Blue Cliff Record.* The compilation of his teachings in the *Rinzai Roku* is still a vital text for Zen students.

RŌHATSU   (J.)   Literally, the eighth day of the twelfth month,

when the enlightenment of Shakyamuni Buddha is commemo-
rated. According to tradition, he had been doing deep meditation
under the bodhi tree when he saw the morning star and had a
profound awakening. Rōhatsu sesshin, usually held in most Zen
monasteries and centers from the evening of November 30
through the morning of December 8, is the most rigorous and
demanding retreat of the year.

RŌSHI   (J.)   Literally, venerable or old master. In the Rinzai tradition it is reserved for one who has undergone long years of strenu-
ous training, has manifested deep insight, maturity, and leader-
ship, and has received the seal of Dharma transmission.

SAHĀ   (S.)   Literally, tolerable, it refers to the world humans in-
habit.

SAIGYŌ   A Japanese poet (1118–1190) who brought new vitality to
the conventions of court poetry. He became a monk at the age of
twenty-two, abandoning a post in the imperial guard, and lived
in secluded mountain huts, writing and making pilgrimages. His
poems are primarily in the thirty-one-syllable *tanka* or *waka*
form.

SAMĀDHI   (S.)   One-pointed concentration; the state of mind
during deep zazen that is unimpeded and undifferentiating. Phenomena are experienced just as they are, with no interference.

SANGHA   (S. *saṃgha*)   One of the three treasures of Buddhism,
along with Buddha and Dharma. Historically, *Sangha* refers to the
assembly that gathered around Shakyamuni Buddha; the broader
reference is to a community of Buddhist practitioners.

SATORI   *See* kenshō.

SEKIDA, KATSUKI   Author of *Zen Training* and *Two Zen Classics,*
an annotated translation of the *Gateless Gate* and the *Blue Cliff
Record.* Sekida (1893–1983) trained at Empuku-ji under Tesshū
Kōzuki and at Ryūtaku-ji under Sōen Nakagawa. He taught at the
Honolulu and Maui zendōs from 1965 to 1970, and at the London
Zen Society from 1970 to 1972.

SENZAKI, NYOGEN   The first Zen monk to live in the United
States, Senzaki (1876–1958) was a student of Sōyen Shaku. He
came to the West Coast in 1905, settling first in San Francisco and
later in Los Angeles. *Nyogen* means "like a phantasm" and is de-

rived from the concluding verse of the *Diamond Sutra;* he spoke of himself "as a lone cloud floating freely in the blue sky," on a "transient stay." After spending nearly two decades working at odd jobs in virtual obscurity, he began to teach; his "Mentorgarten Zendo" in Los Angeles opened in 1931.

SESSHIN   (J.) Literally, to collect or join *(setsu)* the heart-mind *(shin),* sesshin is a period of three, five, or seven days during which students singlemindedly engage in zazen (meditation). Strict silence is maintained throughout. In Rinzai communities, a daily teishō, or Dharma talk, is given by the teacher or a senior student, and dokusan is conducted two or three times a day.

SHAKU, SŌYEN (OR SŌEN)   A Dharma heir of Kōsen Imakita, Kōgaku Sōyen Shaku (1859–1919) took a great interest in Western culture and philosophy. He was the first Zen master to visit the United States from Japan. He addressed the World's Parliament of Religions in Chicago in 1893, and then in 1905 made a second visit, one even more important to the development of Zen practice in the West. He stayed for nearly a year at the home of Mrs. Alexander Russell in San Francisco, giving frequent talks on Buddhism at the request of his hostess, and addressing audiences on both coasts, before making a European tour. His students D. T. Suzuki and Nyogen Senzaki carried on his transmission of Zen to the West.

SHAKUHACHI   (J.)   A bamboo flute often associated with Zen.

SHAKYAMUNI   (S. Śākyamuni)   The name by which Siddhārtha Gautama came to be known (literally, Sage of the Śākyas). *See* Buddha.

SHIKISHI   (J.)   A square panel for calligraphy.

SHIKOKU   An island in Japan with many temples and shrines, known particularly for its pilgrimage circuit of eighty-eight stations.

SHIN DYNASTY (C. CH'ING)   A reign in China from 1619 to 1912.

SHŌGEN-JI   A monastery in Gifu Prefecture founded by Kanzan Egen in the fourteenth century.

SŌTŌ   (J.; C. Tsao-tung)   One of the five schools of Zen that developed in China during the T'ang dynasty. The Sōtō and Rinzai

Schools are the most widely practiced forms of Zen in modern-day Japan and the West. The Sōtō tradition was established by Tōzan Ryōkai (C. Tung-shan Liang-chieh) and his student Sōzan Honjaku (C. Ts'ao-shan Pen-chi); it was brought to Japan by Eihei Dōgen. In the Sōtō School, *shikantaza,* or just sitting, is the principal way of practice.

SHUNYATA   (S. *śūnyatā;* J. *kū*)   Literally, emptiness or voidness, but not in a dualistic or nihilistic sense. To experience shunyata is to realize that all composite things are fundamentally devoid of any fixed condition or substance; hence, to experience them as they are, with no conceptual or preferential shadings. Shunyata is the key teaching in the *Prajñāpāramitā-sūtras,* the best known of which are the *Diamond Sūtra* and the *Heart Sūtra.*

SŪTRA   (S.)   Literally, the thread upon which the jewels of Shakyamuni Buddha's discourses were strung. There are said to be more than ten thousand of these texts. The sūtras written in Pali were based on an early form of Buddhist teaching, which developed into sūtras written in Sanskrit. Much of the Sanskrit canon was translated into Chinese and Tibetan. Relatively few sūtras have been translated into English. Each begins with the phrase "Thus have I heard," the purported narrator being Shakyamuni Buddha's student Ānanda, although sūtras were compiled and continued to be written long after the Buddha's death.

SUZUKI, DAISETZ TEITARŌ   A student of Sōyen Shaku, D. T. Suzuki (1870–1966) became one of the most widely known figures in the transmission of Zen to the West. He first came to the United States in 1897 to help edit Dr. Paul Carus's journal *The Open Court;* he remained until 1909 before returning to Japan. He again traveled to the United States in 1936, and during the 1950s he taught at Columbia University. A prolific author, he wrote more than one hundred thirty books in English and Japanese.

SUZUKI, SŌCHŪ   (1921–1990)   Practiced at Ryūtaku-ji and became one of Sōen Nakagawa's Dharma heirs. After Sōen Rōshi retired, he was installed as abbot of Ryūtaku-ji.

TAKUHATSU   (J.)   Literally, holding a (begging) bowl; the monastic practice of earning a livelihood while training in humility and gratitude. Walking from house to house asking for alms, the monks provide the laity an opportunity to practice charity. They wear traditional straw hats that cover their faces; thus the one who is giving and the one who is receiving are anonymous.

TANAHASHI, JIMMY   A son of Shūbin Tanahashi, Nyogen Senzaki's disciple. Mentally handicapped, he was unable to speak at all; Senzaki taught him to recite "The Four Great Vows."

TANAHASHI, SHŪBIN   Nyogen Senzaki's principal disciple and a very close friend; the mother of Jimmy.

TATHĀGATA   (S.)   *Tathatā* means thusness, things as they are, or suchness. Tathāgata may be translated "thus-come, thus-gone," referring to one who has attained buddhahood. In the sūtras, *Tathāgata* is a term used by Shakyamuni Buddha to refer to himself or to other buddhas.

TEISHŌ   (J.)   A Zen master's formal presentation of the Dharma to the assembly, usually based on a traditional kōan from such compilations as the *Gateless Gate,* the *Blue Cliff Record,* or the *Book of Equanimity.*

TENZO   (J.)   The person in charge of the kitchen at a monastery.

TŌFUKU-JI   A monastery in Kyōto, founded by Shōichi Kokushi; one of the headquarters of the Rinzai School.

TOKUSAN SENKAN   (J.; C. Te-shan Hsuan-chien)   Tokusan (ca. 781–867) appears in cases 13 and 28 of the *Gateless Gate* and in case 4 of the *Blue Cliff Record.* The famous story about him concerns his meeting with an old woman in a teahouse; she brought him to understand that his renowned scholarship regarding the *Diamond Sūtra* had not enabled him to grasp its deep meaning.

TORA YA YA!   Literally, "triangle," referring to the Three Treasures: Buddha, Dharma, and Sangha. A phrase from "The Great Compassionate Dharani" (which begins "Namu kara tan nō"), chanted in the Japanese transliteration of the Sanskrit during morning and other services.

TOSOTSU JŪETSU   (J.; C. Tou-shuai T'sung-yueh)   Zen Master Tosotsu (1044–1091) is best known for his "three barriers" kōan, number 47 of the *Gateless Gate.*

TŌZAN RYŌKAI   (J.; C. Tung-shan Liang-chieh)   Tōzan (807–869) studied with many well-known teachers, including Nansen Fugan (C. Nan-ch'uan P'u-yuan), Isan Reiyū (C. Kuei-shan Ling-yu), and Ungan Donjō (C. Yun-yen T'an-sheng). His own students were numerous; among his twenty-six Dharma heirs were Sōzan Honjaku (C. Ts'ao-shan Pen-chi), with whom he is regarded as founder of the Sōtō School, and Ungo Dōyo (C. Yun-chu Tao-ying). Tōzan is also renowned in the Rinzai School for his teaching of "the Five Ranks," illustrating the dynamic functioning of Dharma. Clear insight into the Five Ranks is considered the culmination of kōan training in Rinzai Zen. Tōzan is encountered in case 43 of the Blue Cliff Record.

UMMON BUN'EN   (J.; C. Yun-men Wen-yen)   Ummon (864–949) was the Dharma heir of Seppō Gison (C. Hsueh-feng I'ts'un) and had more than sixty successors himself. Founder of the Ummon School, he used words in a vivid and dynamic way; no other master's sayings are encountered as frequently as his, in the Gateless Gate (cases 15, 16, 21, 39, and 48) and particularly in the Blue Cliff Record (cases 6, 8, 14, 15, 22, 27, 34, 39, 47, 50, 54, 60, 62, 77, 83, 86, 87, and 88). Many of his responses (often to questions he himself posed) are renowned as "one-word barriers."

UNGAN DONJŌ   (J.; C. Yun-yen T'an-sheng)   Ungan (781–841) left home when still quite young and began his training under Hyakujō Ekai (C. Pai-chang Huai-hai). After Hyakujō's death, Ungan became the student (and eventual Dharma heir) of Yakusan Igen (C. Yao-shan Wei-yen). He is met in cases 70, 72, and 89 of the Blue Cliff Record.

UPĀSAKA, UPĀSIKĀ   (S.)   Layman, laywoman.

VAIROCANA   (S.; J. Dainichi)   The protective deity pictured as the luminous manifestation of the cosmos in esoteric Buddhism.

WAKA   (J.)   Literally, Japanese-style poetry. Often used interchangeably with tanka (a short poem), composed of units of five, seven, five, seven, and seven syllables.

YAMAKAWA, SŌGEN   The present abbot of Shōgen-ji.

YAMAMOTO, GEMPŌ   (1865–1961)   The Zen master from whom Sōen Nakagawa received Dharma transmission, Gempo Yamamoto was abbot of Ryūtaku-ji and was held in the highest esteem not only within the Rinzai Zen establishment but among government officials and the laity. He played an important role in Japan's decision to surrender at the end of World War II.

ZAZEN (J.) Literally, sitting Zen. The practice of sitting still in an alert posture (usually in some form of the lotus, or cross-legged, posture), in which the attention is at once one-pointed and diffuse, focused on the breath and aware of things just as they are.

ZAZENKAI (J.) A Zen sitting group composed primarily of laypersons.

ZEN (J.) Transliteration of the Sanskrit *dhyāna* and the Chinese *ch'an*. Sometimes translated as meditation, the term also refers to the Zen Buddhist schools and practice, as well as to the views and culture developed through Zen practice. Zen is both something one does and something one is.

ZENDŌ (J.) The hall or large room where zazen is practiced in a group.

ZEN STUDIES SOCIETY Established in 1956 in New York City to support the efforts of D. T. Suzuki. In 1965 when Eido Shimano arrived in New York, he revitalized the organization, which now maintains two practice centers: the New York Zendō Shōbō-ji in New York City and International Dai Bosatsu Zendō Kongō-ji in the Catskill Mountains, New York State.